A GAMEFISHER'S YEAR

By the same author

Every Boy's Game Fishing, Stanley Paul
Game Fishing, Stanley Paul
An Introduction to Trout, Sea Trout and Salmon Fishing, Collins
The Art of Trout Fishing, Oliver and Boyd
The Art of Beginning Fishing, Oliver and Boyd (with John Nixon)
Lochs and Rivers of Scotland, Rainbird (with Moray McLaren)

A Gamefisher's Year

WILLIAM B. CURRIE

I do not know much about gods; but I think that the river
Is a strong brown god – sullen, untamed and intractable,
. . . .
His rhythm was present in the nursery bedroom,
In the rank ailanthus of the April dooryard,
In the smell of grapes on the autumn table,
And the evening circle in the winter gaslight.
The river is within us . . . .

T. S. ELIOT

PELHAM BOOKS

First published in Great Britain by
PELHAM BOOKS LTD
26 Bloomsbury Street
London, W.C.1
1969

7207 0248 8

Set and printed in Great Britain by Tonbridge Printers Ltd,
Peach Hall Works, Tonbridge, Kent, in Baskerville eleven on
twelve point, and bound by James Burn at Esher, Surrey

Acknowledgements

Much of this book is drawn from the material of articles published over the last five years in game fishing and other sporting magazines in Britain. Specifically I have to thank the editors of *The Field, The Scottish Field, The Shooting Times, Angling, Creel* (now incorporated in *Angling*). Some of the articles also derive from my own magazine, *Rod and Line*.

W.B.C.

Contents

8

Preface

This book is a kind of diary, but one which is very far from being a mere record of events in any one angling year. It is, rather, a diary which tries to present the essence of one man's fishing over several recent seasons. As a record it traces the movement of game fishing through the changing year from spring salmon sport to summer trouting and autumn fishing; as a record it traces the author's movements throughout Scotland; but more important, this diary moves from the experiences recorded into discussion of sport with game fish, into suggestions for new tactics and reconsideration of old ones, and, at places, it moves into speculation about game fishing as a gripping facet of human behaviour and a strikingly interesting aspect of the use of leisure time. Thus, the book attempts to be both an objective work and a highly personal record written by a keen gamefisher of the sixties. If a proportion of the author's dedication to the sport and the immense pleasure he derives from it are communicated to the reader the book will have been successful, but if the reader finds in it, ideas about fishing which help him, in turn, to fish better or to focus more clearly on problems of conservation and management of game fishing, the book will have a double justification.

WILLIAM B. CURRIE

Edinburgh

Illustrations

Introduction:
A Realistic Portrait of Scottish Fishing

You can easily sit back in an armchair in the club and think about Scottish fishing, dreaming up visions of the unfished wilderness with Landseer mists swirling round romantic peaks. It is easy, but it is wrong. It is almost as easy to be cynical about present-day game fishing in Scotland. Numbers have increased, there is more commercial exploitation than ever, and certain aspects of the sport have disappointed many anglers. But cynical dismissal of Scottish game fishing is as wrongheaded as romantic dreaming of Edwardian plenty. The real game fishing state of Scotland is very different. Indeed, I wonder whether many anglers realise just how much a new order of things has established itself.

Let's begin with Sutherland. In recent years a major effort was made by a local tourist association, working in conjunction with the county Development Officer (part of Town and Country Planning) and backed by the Scottish Tourist Board. The county was surveyed by a team of experts and all the available game fishing was listed and classified. At the same time, estates which had never before considered the possibility were encouraged to make fishings available to visiting anglers, clubs were started in several centres to administer fishings in their area and fishings were advertised.

The survey revealed some interesting statistics. On an average summer day before the survey, 750 anglers were fishing throughout the county of Sutherland. On analysis this could be shown to be a very sparse distribution of anglers indeed. Sutherland has some 400 trout lochs in the average-to-good class and a vast number of inferior waters offering trout fishing throughout the county. There were 150 Hotel boats on Sutherland lochs in 1962–63. In addition there are salmon and sea trout lochs and salmon and sea trout rivers. Distribute 750 anglers over this water and you may have two anglers fishing each accessible loch and a sprinkling of fishers on other waters. This could hardly be called overfishing.

With effort on the proprietors' part, on the local and national Tourist Boards' part and, not least on the part of the local angling clubs, Sutherland fishing now carries nearer 1,000 summer anglers per day and the feeling of underfishing – in some cases serious underfishing of trout lochs prevails. This underfishing can only lead to decline. In the Scottish Highlands where waters are, generally speaking, acid, the most important consideration in fishery management is population control. Underfishing, coupled with spawning facilities leads to gross overpopulation of lochs and decline of quality and size of the stock.

In Caithness, just over the Sutherland border a striking piece of fishery reclamation has been undertaken by the Hon. Robin Sinclair at Lochdhu Lodge Hotel. He has opened up one of the family shooting lodges near Altnabreac as a sporting hotel and in addition to good grouse shooting over pointers and stalking, and salmon fishing on the Thurso the hotel offers trout fishing on a chain of lochs which are under strict, and far sighted, management principles.

Firstly, each loch has its spawning restricted so that a stable population might be achieved. By returns from a water over several seasons the potential harvest of trout such a loch might yield per acre is calculated and re-stocking, or de-stocking appropriate to the water is carried out. In one loch an average of 1 lb. 12 oz. has been reached. In others an average of 1 lb. and close to this figure has been achieved. A striking experiment in trout feeding in one loch on the hotel doorstep has been undertaken and there is evidence that it has solved part of the underfeeding problem common in acid environments. Slaughterhouse waste, a flake meal substance in its dried form, is scattered daily on the loch at certain times of the season – usually early in the year before the natural food migration from deep to shallow water has taken place. The trout thus find food directly, or food encouraged by the nitrogenous fertilisation of the material put into the loch, and they gain weight and condition quickly.

The development of sporting hotels in Scotland is often

stimulated by a county fishery survey, as has happened in Sutherland, or sometimes it is the result of initiative and fore-sight of hoteliers themselves. Generally speaking, the bigger the unit and the wider the variety of fishing offered, the better the scheme operates. Choosing the largest hotel sporting estate in Scotland as an example, Benmore Estates in Sutherland and Ross combine good salmon fishing with a varied bill of hill trout fishing, running their hotel accommodation in the best traditions of a sporting house-party. This has become a standard for fishery development, and for hotel accommodation for the fishery fraternity throughout Scotland.

This type of fishery development is not confined to the Highlands. The Cally Estates in Gatehouse of Fleet have recently developed their excellent range of hill loch fishing, and sea trout and salmon fishing on the Fleet as a single hotel sporting unit. Here again careful watch is kept on the harvest of trout yielded per acre on the lochs and steps are taken to maintain quality of catch rather than allow the fishing to reach a state of natural equilibrium in which myriads of tiddlers age, but never grow large.

What many visitors to Scotland may not realise yet is that in the new developments in Caithness, Sutherland, and Ross (the development most recently undertaken) several important new fishing clubs with ticket waters with good fishing have emerged. Ten years ago one had to seek out proprietors of fishings in Sutherland and make arrangements for trout fishing over their waters. Sometimes proprietors were Londoners, or absentees of another sort, and it was hard either to rent fishing, or acquire permission for a day or so on the lochs. Now, to take Lochinver as an excellent example, a local angling club has been formed and day tickets are offered covering some 30 named lochs and other lochans, and for only 7s 6d per day a visitor may roam the Assynt hills fishing the waters scattered over one of the most beautiful parishes in Scotland. A similar, if less ambitious scheme operates at Scourie in Sutherland. At Lairg, Loch Shin has been developed for trout fishing by the local angling club, assisted by the North of Scotland Hydro Board who own the fishings. Boats have been put on the loch radically increasing the numbers of fishers who can drift the waters of this excellent Highland loch, and an unlimited number of banks can be accommodated. On a loch with so much wild shoreline, bank fishing is virtually unlimited in scope.

On the fringe of Scotland, the outer Hebrides, where some very exciting fishing is to be had, clubs are again forming the nucleus of new management of fishings. Stornaway now has ticket water available and throughout Lewis three clubs now have water available on above average trout lochs for visitors' fishing. In the northern margins of Scotland (although the islanders themselves form a little separate 'kingdom') Orkney and Shetland fishing is well organised, well managed and available to visitors. Shetland merely say they have 'over 100 lochs, burns and sea lochs' available for 15 shillings per week. Orkney has the only really free trout fishing in the British Isles, but even there a vigorous new era of management is under way with analysis and re-stocking taking place in all the principal waters. A local Orkney Trout Fishing Association carries out this work and *asks* for a subscription of 7s 6d from those who fish its waters. Only a cad would refuse; many anglers give generous donations to so enthusiastic a group.

I believe that a new willingness to travel far to good fishing is abroad among visiting anglers to Scotland, and among Scots anglers themselves. This is partly because fishing too near hotels and ticket centres are all too often fished hard, but it is also because it is part of the urge of angling to roam into the wilderness. Scotland may be organising its resources much more efficiently, but it is still a country where the man who likes to feel alone with his fish can do so.

I firmly believe that anglers must walk if they are to find good hill loch fishing. Firstly, permission is easier to obtain for a remote loch, since other guests of the hotel or lodge will be unwilling to walk if they have easier fishing available. In Western Inverness-shire with a good fishing companion I had an ideal day at trout one June. We took our cars up a small spate valley to the farm, and from there set out to scale the eight hundred foot face of the hill which shut in the glen. It took an hour of puffing and blowing to cross the ridge, but the Red Loch, our destination soon shone before us. No one had fished it that year. We set up our rods and went off in opposite directions, fishing the rippled water right into the heather. From the first fish it was clear that the trout were not small.

They ran well up to a pound in weight and from time to time one would be pulled or splashed at by a marvellous trout far in excess of this weight. Two of a pound and a quarter were taken, fighting well, then a low cloud came down in mist to make the Red Loch as eerie a place as a stage manager could devise.

We might well have taken it for granted that a mist plus a falling wind make for hopeless conditions, but we fished on, and after a pause in the rise the trout came back on to the feed. My friend hooked a splendid fish of 2 lb. 2 oz. My best was 1 lb. 7 oz. It was trouting in the first quality, and in the swirling mist, quite unforgettable. We carried down ten fish, returning all the others. and I would say that bag was as good a sight as any hill loch could yield. (See Chapter Thirty-five).

In many senses, Scotland is still unexplored from the angling point of view. I do not mean that waters have not been fished; I mean that anglers of this generation have not yet re-discovered much of the fishing available. Why is it that Charles McLaren, going back to the boyhood fishings he had known on Loch Maree, at Kinlochewe, in 1960 was the first man to catch a salmon in spring on the loch for many years? Simply, he was the first man to follow up what the record books show, that anglers who knew where to put their flies in April and May found the head of Maree a good spring salmon producer. But what about the head of Loch Hope, Loch Assynt, Loch Stack, Loch Sheil? Who fishes there in April and May? I can answer this in part – no one fishes Hope these days, yet the keepers in the area remember the fishing tenants taking spring fish on fly. I myself have met anglers of my father's generation who took good bags off the head of Hope in April fishing in the twenties and thirties. Has the war made us forget?

Under-fishing is one of the faults of Scottish management, and although it is being rectified, a great deal must still be done to make fishing available to visitors. It must be cheap, since many of to-day's keenest anglers are men of modest means, quite unlike the tenants who used to take estates in the north earlier this century. What should a man expect to pay in Scotland, then, for trout fishing? Fishing without a boat or a loch should not cost more than 10s per day and that only in the best cases. This is really a general rule and does not cover special ponds and lochs where big rainbow or where sea trout or salmon are to be taken. With a boat a maximum of about £2 per day for the best trouting is reasonable, with most of the fishings falling between 17s and £1 10s for a boat. Many good hotels include trouting in their tariff. Lochdhu for example in Caithness offers really good trouting included in a tariff of £18 18s od per week. For sea trout fishing, the quality of the water dictates the rate. No one grudges the £7 or £8 per day for a boat on Stack with its magnificently big sea trout. However, £2 per day is nearer the usual charge for sea trout fishing on lochs. Salmon fishing is harder to categorise. It runs the range of the occasionally good at a few shillings per day, to the splendid beats of top class rivers rented by the month at what almost seems to be a statement of the national annual average salary! Yet, even on Spey, £2 per day for hotel water is reasonably obtainable and association water is available, if somewhat popular when the runs are on. Keep three figures in your mind when budgeting; trout, £1 per day with boat, sea trout £2 per day with boat (loch) or on a reasonable night beat of a river. Salmon £2 per day upwards on reasonable water whose returns are known.

A short tourist bibliography might be useful. No one can plan a fishing holiday without *Scotland for Fishing*, available from the Tourist Board and bookstalls 3s 6d. *Where to Fish*, published by *The Field* is a well known travelling angler's companion, priced 21s. Many very useful area guides are now becoming available in Scotland. *Sutherland, Ross* and *Cromarty, Inverness-shire, Caithness, Orkney & Shetland* and *Argyll* are now on the market either through the Tourist Board or the Highland and Islands Board, but all are available in tackle shops or good bookstalls. Remember also the small but helpful *Border Angling Guide* for Tweedside and that area. Finally, for the angler who wants more than a list of places and prices, a fat and detailed account of the resources of Scottish loch and river fishing will shortly be available – *Lochs and Rivers of Scotland*, by Moray McLaren and William B. Currie, published by Rainbirds.

CHAPTER ONE

Types of Non-Springer

In the earlier part of the spring salmon season – that part the poets call midwinter spring – the salmon fisher is likely to hook a remarkable variety of fish, takable and untakable. The pattern is usually like this – January: the odd springer, but three clear classes of untakable fish – large kelts, small kelts and rawners. These last three are strikingly different from each other in appearance (and performance). In addition in January or February one often takes a winter fish, a not uncommon early spring phenomenon. These five types of fish, one springer and four non-springers represent the wide and interesting population of fish a water like the Tay may yield to a rod in the early spring.

Kelts come as no surprise, but what is interesting is the variety of physical types they show. I have seen fifty seven kelts taken in one day to three hard working rods on Tay. The large kelts are nearly all female fish, some heavy fish in the twenties of pounds. These female kelts are usually darkish in colour, vigorous and hard fighting. Some leap in the fight; some take line hard twice in the fight; some, if foul hooked, will take you two hundred and fifty yards downstream as one did me early in February. Everyone thought it was a fresh thirty pounder. How we swore! In their prime what magnificent fish they must have been, and even in decline, how powerful. They are usually quite free from disease, and the normal degree of winter damage one sees (apart from usual emaciation) is tail wear from the redds. These particular kelts disappear by the end of February (I hope they get back to the sea) and they are replaced by a much smaller, brighter fish without half their character.

The small kelts of the early spring river are normally bright tinny silver. Weighing at a guess around five pounds, they can give the impression of being fresh fish when they glint in the water, but any experienced angler knows the weak pulsating fight of one of these small creatures. They look clear, but have maggot ridden gills and their thin bodies sometimes give the idea of eels rather than grilse. These small fish inhabit the streams usually and set up what might be described as a kelt hierarchy in the main pools of Tay. It is a grading of size, from five pounders in the streams to twenty pounders in the pool dubs. It is a grading of colour from silvery small fish to darker and more highly coloured fish; it is a grading of power from weak little kelts to some taking ten minutes to bring into the bank.

The rawners (or baggots) of Tay are remarkable fish. Seventeen, to twenty pounds is a normal size. These fine big hens have, for reasons unknown, not shed their spawn and they may never do so. A typical catch was an eighteen pounder, bluish on the back, purplish silver on the deep flanks and off-white belly heavy with spawn. During the hand tailing no spawn extruded but the fish was clearly ripe. I have seen a number of hens in this condition, but this one made me think of Menzies's statement that there is often no physical reason why a baggot should not shed its ova; they could be stripped by hand. This particular one seemed less likely to shed its spawn (although I did not try) and an examination of the vent suggested that it was completely unbroken and tight. The flesh of the fish felt firm and the general appearance was good although the colour was dark.

Early one February I took a small winter fish. It took a devon and gave me a good fast fight. Twice I saw it during the fight and in each case I had a glimpse of a high back and a well shaped, but dull coloured, little fish. It was duly tailed out and presented a very ticklish problem of identification. Three of us decided that this fish looked fresh, was clearly unspawned, but not mature in spawn, and had many of the characteristics of the springer but with two features of the kelt. Firstly it was a darkish fish, although with a splendidly white belly. Secondly it had maggots in its gills. We decided to kill the fish and do an autopsy. This bankside examination came as a relief to me, since one of the haunting fears I have is to return a fresh fish – or to kill an unclean one. I remember vividly the curses of a ghillie on Spey when he discovered a dead fresh fish in the bottom of a pool where a timid guest, well warned not to kill kelts, had returned a very tired springer!

The autopsy showed the milts of the salmon to be about two inches long, completely immature. The vent was unbroken, of course. This was, internally, what I would have taken a springer to be. The flesh was red, but perhaps not so well laminated with fat as the fresh springer. The weight was only eight pounds. A springer of the same length would have been about nine, I estimated.

This little fish may have been several months in the river, and the gill maggots it carried may well have been acquired during its stay. I dismissed the possibility of such a small fish being a second spawner, although now that I have discussed the matter with several knowledgeable anglers I am not so sure that weight is necessarily any indication of this. A grilse of five pounds may spawn and return as a small fish of eight pounds, although I grant that these weights are unusual.

Tay brings fish in to its waters in every month of the year. The Loch Tay stock may be running up through the middle reaches (where my fishings nearly all take place in spring) as early as the end of October. November runners are known *in Loch Tay*, and these are spawners for the following autumn. Many winter fish could be of that vintage but merely salmon which did not want to move further than the middle pools of the river. Salmon may be allowed to have idiosyncracies too.

On Tweed in the early season, one may hook full fish which are very fresh looking and are virtually ready to spawn, and in my opinion, if returned, would do so. Some local clubs ensure that such fish are treated (as they probably ought to be in law) as unclean, although to the eye they look like springers. In Tweed and Teviot I have seen clean little fish of the eight pound order, very blue on the back and very firm in the flesh immature, grilse-like salmon, which locals call blue-backs. These fish seem to appear in the river in the early season and they disappear before the spring run proper advances. I honestly suspect this theory. I expect these little fish run far up into hill burns and there they lie undetected until the spawning of the autumn. Salmon may move downstream because of floods, but I would not subscribe easily to a theory that they voluntarily moved away while they were still unspawned.

This chapter is, of course, not a plea that we should kill unclean fish, nor even that we should take the benefit of the doubt to work on our side. It is really to draw attention to the somewhat complicated and surprisingly varied population of fish a single beat of a large river may have. By the end of March, springers will outnumber kelts, if our records are right. After April it will be an oddity to take a kelt – although I have seen one taken in July in Faskally Dam, and I have seen many May kelts in various waters.

CHAPTER TWO

. . . And One Springer

Having a beat on a river like the Tay allows you to see the movement of the whole game fishing year at its most panoramic aspect. Tay begins fishing in January and finishes in October. There would be every reason to expect that, if you fished from the end of the season through the winter until the 'spring' fishings of the next year you would still take daily, fresh run salmon. Tay is a prolific river, an endless cycle of natural activity. Its fascinating wealth of fish may be gauged from a quite remarkable day I had on it one season, on my first day out, in January 1967.

I should say that my usual fishings on the Tay are near Caputh, that is, about 12 river miles from Perth. This is on the fat lower section of the river, although some would say the really fat beats were all below the Isla mouth. I am about three miles above this. Nevertheless, we have three pools on our 2,000 yards of water, and one of them, Burnbane, is a most impressive piece of water, half a mile long, with a superb head-stream of some three hundred yards followed by a flat gravel-bottomed tail gliding for about the same distance. My heart never fails to lift when I breast the ridge on the steep south bank and I see through the trees sixty feet below me the exciting stream of the main pool.

January fishing is patchy in most seasons and there are always plenty of kelts to contend with. For our opening day I brought up a very keen fisher – you know, the sort of man to whom even a kelt is a big fishing thrill. Like many young fishers he is rather cock-sure of himself and in the car as we drove up he wagered that he could take a kelt on his first cast. We accepted. The offer of pints all round seemed a courtesy rather than a bet.

It took Mike two casts to hook a fish. I was slower. It took me three casts. We were playing our first fish of the year, albeit kelts. To some this would be an uninspiring prospect (one of my colleagues cannot handle kelts; they revolt him) but to us that day it was the beginning of the new year and to feel the rod bending so soon – and in both cases so well – for Mike's fish was a baggot about eighteen pounds in weight – was agreeable. We returned our fish made a few remarks about the wager and began fishing proper, on what turned out to be the most fantastic piece of fishing activity I have ever experienced.

We caught twenty kelts in the first hour and a half. Some were heavy fish of well up into the teens of pounds; some were five pound, slashing, clean little silvery grilse kelts. To make it more interesting we set up fly tackle and fished Tweed-style Garry dogs that we had tied up specially for the occasion. Twelve kelts were accounted for by fly, and when you add to this the pike-like swirls of near misses, and strangely enough, the beautiful head and tail takes of some of the offers, it was an hour or so of continuous activity. My own rod was seldom straight. A fish was no sooner tailed, unhooked and released than the fly was boiled at by another fish, the line would tighten and the arch of the rod would announce that it was all happening once again.

But, we asked ourselves at lunch time, where were the fresh fish? Our beat usually produces a brace or two of fresh springers in January with occasional days of red letter catches when we are presented with a batch of fresh salmon stopping with us in the main pool for a day or so. The previous season we had no January fish (our days at least) and it was February before things began to be productive. We had always numbers of kelts, but never anything like this.

By lunch time we had returned thirty-five kelts and had not touched a springer. My arms were beginning to ache. Mike was in ecstacy. Wasn't he disappointed that we had not touched a springer, we asked. Not a bit of it. Whenever the rod top went over into a salmon of any kind, he argued, he had that old familiar feeling, 'Into him!' and this to him was sport. I reflected that that 'old familiar feeling' was all too unfamiliar on many salmon fishing days.

We crossed to the other bank and began the hard labour of

fishing. It *was* hard labour. The total of returned kelts grew, and reached the upper forties and my own spirits dropped somewhat as this circus went on – kelt after kelt. To help my depression, the rain came on harder, the wind rose and it became very cold. I found at one stage that I could not control my fingers enough to unhook kelts. In a numb state I trudged to where Mike was again trying the fly on the stream at the head of the main pool. Reflecting that the water was far too fast for a springer, I offered Mike my Ambassadeur/LRH 2 outfit and invited him to try it while I took over his fly rod for ten minutes and got the circulation moving again. Mike agreed. He walked to the side of the shingle thirty yards below me, cast out a silver/gold Milbro T bait (a spoon) and was fast into a fish.

I watched the rod top moving and thought it looked a good fish. Must be a big kelt, I thought. Mike was coping well and indicated that he would manage the landing himself. Suddenly he shouted 'Springer!'. Now I should say that he had done this twice before during the day and I had twice run in waders to land the fish only to find out it was another kelt. This time I called 'Fiddlesticks! It's a kelt. I can see its tail from here!'

True enough, a great tail kept appearing out of the boils and splashes. Then, with what seemed remarkable haste, Mike reached down into the water, picked up his fish and ran like a rabbit back from the river on to the shingle. Clutched in his hand was the most magnificent salmon, eighteen pounds, silver, burnished, high backed and everything else that a fresh Tay fish is in the spring. It was the finest salmon I have ever seen for proportions, colour, sheen.

This was Mike's twenty first landing of the day! Twenty kelts and assorted baggots and then this superb springer. By the end of the day the three rods fishing that beat had returned fifty seven kelts, and had killed one springer. To many this may seem a distressing record. But let me put this day's hard labour into perspective. I have been fishing for salmon consistently all over Scotland since 1947 and on various waters I have had 'plague' days of kelts. But this was different. I have never in one day had such fish playing activity . . . never even in sea fishing. These kelts were hard and good fighters in many cases. Many took line twice. Many leapt. Never have I had a

25

day's activity like this. And it does something for you. It works as a kind of purge. The sheer hunger one has for the bending rod is completely worked out. What you look forward to for the rest of the season is challenging, thoughtful salmon fishing.

And of course there was one other effect. On the morning after, my arms, legs and back ached as if I had spent my day not fishing, but engaging in all-in wrestling.

I remember filling in my beat return for this January day. 'One salmon, 18 lb. ...' What that report conceals is remarkable.

CHAPTER THREE

The Changing Pattern of Salmon Runs

Probably the hardest of all tasks in the game fishing world is the collection of statistics and the assessment of those figures with some sort of objectivity. The harvest of salmon in Scotland is shared by so many people – proprietors of rod fishings, netsmen in the estuaries and netsmen round the coasts – and each party has more than one good reason for not allowing too many of his salmon returns to be made public. In trying to find evidence for or against a trend in salmon runs one faces an almost insuperable task.

Over several seasons recently, I made several fact-finding trips throughout Scotland and I wrote to a number of people intimately connected with salmon fishings on most of our noted waters trying to find out if the persistent complaint of anglers was true that salmon runs in Scotland are swinging away from the spring to summer and autumn. I tried not to allow any one season to affect the findings disproportionately, but where full records of a water are not kept, or are not available, I have sifted angling opinion for my evidence. Of course, there is no doubt at all, that a disgruntled tenant, a disappointed ghillie or a frustrated owner is liable to distort a situation such as a decline and make it greater or less to suit his argument. A tenant exaggerates a poor spring; an owner looking towards the maintenance of his rents, exaggerates a good one.

The rivers of most interest to us in our survey are mainly the north and east flowing waters of Scotland. It may be that there are some western waters with genuine spring runs, but they are hardly to be compared with northern and eastern waters. Nith and Cree both appear to be improving their spring fishings and there is a good case for regarding Nith as a spring river emergent, but at the moment we must regard it as a water, like other west coast fishings, more noted for the absence of its spring fishing than for early sport, and excelling in summer and autumn runs of some magnitude. The most interesting start we could make on the survey of true spring rivers would seem to be with Thurso, Naver, Brora and Helmsdale.

The records of the Thurso are probably the finest salmon records kept anywhere in this country. They cover a whole river and extend in great detail from the early nineteen twenties to the present day, and in slightly less detail extend back to the mid-nineteenth century. Thus it was possible to take any season or seasons in the past forty years, compare it month by month (or day by day if we had wanted to) with any other period in that time, and obtain a clear picture of the contrasts in salmon runs in terms of catches at least. April is the best spring month on Thurso, taken over the years. May can eclipse April at times; March never does. When May appears to be a better month a close examination of the daily records shows at least one relevant factor – water height – playing a key part. In spring fishing on the Thurso, a fly-only river, high water (more than 10 in. on the gauge at Halkirk Bridge) tends to deter fish from taking. In the later season, water height does not have this material effect on catches. Notice that this explains why catches, which are the index of our run profile in this case, decline in some years in April.

The Thurso records show in recent years that the river is adding a large, and in the case of 1963, 1964 and 1965, a vast grilse and late summer run to its spring fishings. Whether this is a short-lived phenomenon or a pointer to an increase in harvest, time alone will tell. This trend, however, is paralleled on the Brora, and to some extent on the Helmsdale and Naver.

An interesting sidelight on the trends of angling tenants, rather than the trends of fish, appeared on examination of the Thurso records. Few present day tenants are prepared to fish January and February and March. In the twenties, however, the estate gave a bonus to all ghillies fishing the tenants' beats and for every January fish there was a five shilling reward; for every February fish caught, half-a-crown and for every March fish grassed a shilling was paid. The returns for these years in which the incentive scheme operated are significantly higher than later seasons. The old tenants who would at one time fish the river really early caught fish; the ghillies of the twenties caught fish; today only a few locals bother with the very early weeks and no tenants come up before March. Nothing like the true figures for the very early weeks has been recorded since the bonus scheme was dropped.

The Brora river is another water where an owner keeps excellent records. It is also a river where the entire water (like the Thurso) is managed as a whole salmon fishery. Records extending in detail for over twenty-five years give close accounts of the run profile in the river. A general inspection of the figures shows that a peak in spring is usually found in April. In earlier years the bulge appeared sometimes as early as March and continued into April. Usually, the peak runs from late April into May.

The Brora, however, seems to be adding later runs to its spring fishings. In recent years the total harvest of the fishings has increased as a result of this. There is no question of later runs supplanting the earlier ones, but equally, there is no doubt that summer and autumn fishing in recent years has shown a marked trend upwards. In 1964, for example, the summer fishing was strikingly good in late August and September.

On the Naver and Helmsdale I have had to form my opinion from the views of local anglers, river watchers and others intimately connected with the fishings, but I believe the sum of my findings is true to the real situation. On the Naver it would appear that a cycle of some thirty years duration is now well through its revolution. The river has turned from being a water where spring fish were hardly known to being a river with a significant spring run. This in turn has changed in recent years to being a river where the spring run is small and the later fishings have enormously improved. The vast grilse and summer runs of 1963, 1964 and 1965 seem to be supplanting spring fishings, but providing most spectacular sport at times with beats returning twenties and thirties of fish in a day to two rods fishing fly.

The Helmsdale was, earlier this century, a strikingly early and very productive river for spring salmon. A peak in early April running on till May however, has now given way to a later and smaller peak in May and June. What local people call a 'real' spring fishing for the salmon is now rare. There are patches of excellent sport still however in the earlier months, even as early as the beginning of March, but the consistent sport for which the river was famous seems to have changed from March-April to May-June.

Proprietors all over Scotland have outlined to me their own explanations for the change in the character of the salmons runs. The spring decline, where it exists, is explained generally under three clear arguments. Firstly, some maintain that the rainfall pattern is changing and April which was a wet month and a mild one, is now a cold windy drought month and salmon do not run. Secondly, drift netting was not only more extensive than was thought in 1960–61 but was practised surreptitiously before that. Thirdly, that local hazards for spring salmon (which many confidently expect to breed other spring fish) have been greatly increased in recent years because of greater fishing pressure, more spinning rather than fly fishing, and because spring fish lie all season in the upper pools of rivers, exposed longer to the poacher, whether he uses poison, explosives or nets. There is no doubt that these factors all affect fish stocks. How far they are responsible for general run decline is difficult to assess. A plea I met again and again was for a longer weekly close season for netting which would help to off-set the steady netting out of spring fish. Autumn fish run freely into our rivers because the nets are off.

The Aberdeenshire Dee is a noted spring river, but on which two main factors can radically alter the profile of spring runs. If there is little snow, as happens many years, or if there is low water in the early spring or summer, fish either run very quickly through to the eighty miles of upper water where the spawning resources of the river are, or they remain milling round the coast until water comes. The nets in the estuary and the stations round the coast nearby make a disproportionately high killing in such years. Until a careful analysis of the proportionate kills of rods and nets is made, no real conclusion can be drawn here. There is a strong opinion among proprietors of rod fishings, however, that the river is changing and that spring fishing is on the decline. A keen campaign for the development of a hatchery programme is being carried out and river proprietors are anxious to have the weekly netting time curtailed by extending the statutary close hours to forty-eight, and to have the netting season stop in July rather than August. This is an indication that local rather than general conditions are held responsible for the decline in spring fishing on the Dee.

If ever a river needed careful statistical analysis it is the Spey. There are so many individual harvests over such a great length of water that it is impossible in the absence of official figures (they are not released) to be aware of the true total picture. Although I have collected my material on the Spey from a wide variety of sources, spread over the effective fishings of the river, it is still possible to be quite wrong about the pattern of runs in the absence of official figures.

1963 and 1964 for example presented us with a striking contrast in the salmon runs of the Spey. The heavy snowfall of the early months of 1963 gave winter conditions well into the 'spring' fishing season and the runs of salmon appeared to be held back. By mid-April however, a tremendous run of spring fish had arrived and the sport on Spey from Grantown down was, at times, phenomenal. 1964 brought a mild winter and a dry spring and spring runs were poor but over the spring months, one gathers from reports of the productivity of the beats, the spring fishings were well sustained into June, all be it at a modest level. The autumn of 1964 found the river authorities 'satisfied' that a good spawning stock was already on the redds of the tributaries.

Contacts on the Spey have reported to me variously that 1964 was their best individual season (middle Spey); was average (upper middle); was disastrously poor in the spring (lower middle). No one would want to draw firm conclusions from these varied reports. Working from the objective basis of river reports in magazines however, even though we do not have figures for aggregate catches, we do have a rudimentary picture of run distribution. There seems little doubt that some recent springs have produced spring runs later than expected, and there is further information available that summer runs of grilse and small fish are on the increase, but in no sense does the information available justify a view that the spring runs of Spey are declining in favour of later runs.

The picture on Tay is clearer although again the conclusions have been drawn from individual tenant's returns, from word of mouth contact with proprietors, ghillies and from my own fishing. Over the whole year, the Tay is as productive as ever, but a change in the returns is clear. In a typical spring in recent years the season will open early with a better stock of fish in the upper waters, above the Tummel confluence, and in Loch Tay, than the tenants expected, say, ten years ago. When this early fishing is over, – and it may take only a few days of productive fishing on some beats to diminish it considerably – there is a lull in the spring fishing until small fresh runs come in to the river. Formerly, the spring runs were much more of a mass event with a beat enjoying steady fishing over a definable period from February to April. Now the fish run in smaller batches, stay a much shorter time in a beat, and appear to move rapidly through the lower Tay to the upper reaches. Naturally, many anglers blame the hydro-electric board activities. When it is discovered, however, that this pattern is reflected on the Dee, and Tweed systems where there is no hydro-electric interference, the argument loses weight.

The Tay more or less closes down as a salmon river in the mid-summer months, although in recent years an excellent run of grilse has been noted in July and early August. The later summer fishings, however, yield a higher proportion of fresh late fish than formerly. The lower and middle river benefits from this 'back end' run far more than higher beats for the simple reason that the early closing date in mid-October prevents this developing late run reaching upper waters before fishing closes for the season.

More than one experienced Tweed angler has expressed the opinion that if he could choose the months of the year in which to fish the Tweed, fixing his own close season, he would begin serious fishing in mid-September, fish through the excellent autumn runs right into December and continue fishing until the spring runs of fish appeared in February. By April one could argue that one had had the best of the sport until autumn came again.

The current legal season for Tweed fishing begins on 1st February and ends at the end of November. Many of the mid summer months are hardly worth fishing at all for salmon. Tweed is extraordinary. It yields fresh grilse-like fish in mid-

The author tailing out a clean 16-pounder from the Garden Pool of the Aberdeenshire Dee, Comonty Water. The fish took a small Sweep fished on greased line in May

Playing a spring fish on the Earn, Perthshire. Getting well above the fish on a clear bank is an immense advantage to the angler. Mr Ian Calcott is fishing

Fly fishing for June salmon on the small headwaters of the South Esk at Cortachy Castle. The angler, Major Alistair Howman, is using a nine foot six trout rod with small tube flies, on which he has splendid sport in the small stream

November, which are still fresh and grilse-like in February. It brings in genuine springers from December onwards, fish which will not spawn for twelve months, and running even after the springers of new year, comes a run of heavy winter or very late autumn fish ready to spawn and become kelts by April of the new season.

What is a spring run on Tweed? Basically I would say it is a run of eight pounders with tiny roes and not a run of much heavier silvery fish with roes as big as marrows. In autumn the run is much more clearly defined. In recent years great increases in the autumn runs have been noted with the years from 1962 to 1966 outstanding in this way. There is a strong feeling that autumn runs are replacing former spring runs. It is true that there have been local harvests of springers. Sometimes Teviot and Ettrick, principally the latter – the main spring tributary of the system – seem to do better than the parent stream, but in general most anglers would unhesitatingly classify Tweed as an autumn river *par excellence*. Tweed is also seen as having a variable bounty of spring fish and a considerable wealth of spring *fishing*, to make a distinction between total sport with baggots and sport only with small fresh springers.

Tweed suffered early through drift netting and, with the Dee, perhaps suffered worst. This may well have weakened still further the spring run. Certainly the authorities agreed to start rod fishing and netting a fortnight later in 1965 and 1966 to compensate for the loss of stock. It will also, after a study of the runs, be possible to assess whether a natural decline of spring fish has taken place in future years or whether drift netting has decimated the progenitors of the run.

Out of surveying our Scottish salmon fishings for this chapter comes one striking conclusion which is not really about salmon at all. It is that salmon statistics are not kept in full enough detail everywhere for proper statistical judgements to be made about the change in total salmon runs. What do we really know about salmon runs statistically? We count rod catches, some proprietors making a much better job of it than others, and those figures together, with 'secret' netting catches go to the Ministry of Agriculture and Fisheries*. A condensed statement of the total catches appears in the press many months later,

* In Scotland to the Department of Agriculture and Fisheries.

giving meaningless aggregates not tied down to either month or area. Is this all we know about salmon numbers? Are we satisfied not to be able to answer questions like 'When was the probable effect of rainfall on salmon runs last year?' Do we know whether the grilse run was larger than usual, and if so, how much larger it was? On a wider scale, we must be able to tell whether a river has a cycle of peak and dip runs and the time scale of the cycle would be of great assistance in keeping a perspective on fishings. Until we set our minds to counting salmon properly on a statistically respectable basis we shall have to put up with partial and misleading assessments of our stocks. The salmon is one of our great natural resources. Surely we should take the trouble to study the fish by counting and by other means lest we find ourselves faced with a decline in stocks which would have been stemmed had it been properly predicted.

CHAPTER FOUR

The Pursuit of Depth: (1) Fly Fishing

In the spring and autumn of every salmon season I find my attention more and more taken up with what might seem to the layman as a very unimportant matter. I try all kinds of tricks to make a salmon fly sink well, yet still be in control as it fishes over the salmon lie. We have to sink salmon flies in the cold waters of autumn and in the even colder waters of the mid-winter season we call 'spring' salmon time. Salmon will not readily move to a fly presented high in the water over the lie in temperatures of water below 45 deg. F. Don't ask me why. At best I could launch out into a theory about salmon reflex action and temperature. Let's stay practical and say that we have discovered that salmon in cold water take a deep slow fly and that it is very hard indeed to sink the fly effectively in the conditions we meet.

If it strikes you at once that all you have to do is dress a fly on heavy hooks, or dress lead into the fly materials, you are taking a non-fishing view of the matter. A very heavy fly is difficult, and even dangerous to cast, and in the water does not swim properly unless the stream is very fast. Most anglers find that it is necessary to have a heavy silk line to cast out such a fly and they choose a Kingfisher No. 6 or even a No. 7 and, using their heaviest 14 or 15 ft. rod, they manage with some physical effort to cast their fly out sufficiently well to cover the lies.

The heavy silk line, however, has one great drawback, bulk. If you are faced with getting the fly down in a stream of good pace your bulky line will act against you. It will catch the current and, even with better than average line control (mending, etc.), you will find that it is all too easy to have the bulky silk line draw the fly away too quickly from the lie and defeat the deep, slow technique you originally tried to use.

Some years ago I began a series of trials of modern terylene sinking lines. These lines do not have the bulk of silk, yet they have the weight. They can be produced in a wide variety of tapers including forwards tapers with the 'lump' of the line forward as a casting weight. They are also made in conventional double tapers with the 'lump' in the middle of the line. Recently these lines have appeared in two new forms also – level, and detachable casting head form. A level line, as the name suggests, is a line without tapers of any kind. Its end is as thick as its middle. Aero-dynamically, this is not a good thing, but in salmon fishing with a heavy fly and a strong rod and, let it be said, some skill, it should be possible to present this kind of line without too much mess, and the water, with any luck, will do the straightening of the cast and will eventually fish the fly round. The other new line idea is the detachable forward casting head which can be about ten yards long with a very heavy belly behind and a spliced loop at the rod end for attachment to an existing fly line.

I was able to give this detachable casting head a limited test one November on the Tweed and Teviot and again in February and March of the following spring. While the head sank quickly and shot line well, very much as a forward taper would, it was an unpleasant line to fish. Attached to a middle weight line (an HCH Wet Cel AFTM 8), it proved to be an excellent fast sinker and yet still to be capable of being mended to some extent. Attaching this head to a nylon monofilament backing or to some similar fine shooting line may make a phenomenally long casting line, but it is tackle which I regard as distasteful and unfishable.

My trials of this line are by no means over. At present I am rather stuck because I cannot make a supple enough splice between the casting head and the line behind; a varnished splice of silk wrapping is quite useless. It jams in the top ring. I have made splices of silk wrapping with beeswax well worked in and melted with finger friction heat. The result looks as if it would slip through any ring, yet several kelts in spring showed me that the critical point in having a splice jam is as the fish comes in close, towards the tailing or netting stage. The rod is held high and the angle of the line to the rod is made acute. In these conditions even my beeswax covered splice, which felt as supple as rubber, jammed and made me lower the rod top to let it run free. Any experienced angler knows how dangerous that can be in terms of hook hold.

The best all round compromise in fishing a well sunk fly which I have yet discovered is, rather predictably, a Wet Cel (AFTM 10), which seems to slip or cut down through streams and presents no bulk to the pressure of the water. I often fish this with small flies – up to No. 1 salmon size – and I have a special liking for hair wing flies on fine hooks. These flies again provide no excessive resistance to the water and they slip down with the line, yet rise and fan over the lies one wants to fish with a gratifying sensitivity. The Wet Cel is the most sensitive sunk line I have yet fished. Using flies as small as a No. 10 sea trout dressing I have hooked salmon and felt all the thrill of the draw and the knock. The well sunk line does not necessarily rob you of the proper feelings of fly fishing.

A recent line to be run on to one of my salmon reels pleases me immensely. It is the Cortland GAF Sink Tip Taper. About three yards of line in the heavy forward belly, is a Terylene sinking line and the rest of the line is a nylon floater. This is a superb line to cast; it roll casts beautifully (which no other forward taper line I have tried does well), and fishing some of the pools of the Thurso with this sink-tip I found I had distance with depth where I wanted it – at the fly and not at the belly of the line. A great advantage, too, is that the line one hand-lines in is easily shot out again since it floats, whereas a sinking line coils down to the river bottom at your feet.

A logical way to produce weight with small diameter is to build weight into your fly line by running metal into its weave, or as the Gladding *Aquasink* has done, running a soft metal core down the inside of a sinking terylene line. This produces a line which looks like a trout line as far as diameters are concerned, but which has full AFTM10 rating. This thin fast sinking line can cut its way down through streams and fish flies right on to the noses of salmon. In unscrupulous hands it could even be used to sniggle, or grab, salmon by foul hooking. On Tweed there is no doubt that *any* heavy line in the hand of the fish-grabbing fraternity tends to make it easier for snigglers.

37

Only rogues have anything to do with this form of poaching, of course, but we must always be aware that the deeper we fish, the stronger is the chance that our flies could be snatching instruments and our delicately dressed flies become merely decorated grapnels.

Wet Cel now produce two grades of sinking fly line, one labelled 'fast sinking' and the other 'slow sinking'. I have seen fast sinking Wet Cel lines up to AFTM 12, designed for heavy spring or autumn fishing. The rod to handle this very heavy line must be a very well constructed, very robust fourteen or fifteen footer. To use a line like this on, say, your standard thirteen footer will almost certainly wreck it. Even glass of a lighter quality will break if it is asked to handle massively heavy lines like this. We would do well to consult our tackle dealer, or better still, the manufacturer, on how much a given rod can bear.

The pursuit of depth with the fly rod places strains not only on the tackle used; it places strain on the casting technique the angler must use. You cannot lift a very heavy line straight out of the water. The sunk line with twenty yards or so well down can shatter a good cane rod if a powerful backcast is made against the pressure. A necessary part of every cast when you are deep line fishing for salmon is a roll cast. The line is brought back by handlining until only some fifteen to eighteen yards remain in the water. The rod is then raised to the vertical and the line hanging from the top is allowed to droop until it forms a belly almost touching the hand on the butt. The rod is then swept down to the horizontal and the sunk line is rolled up towards the surface of the water – often clearing itself right out in the rolling process. The backcast is now made and the cast carried out in the traditional overhead manner. This, with the excellent shooting qualities of the modern sinking fly line, produces good distance and, because the roll brings the deeply sunk line to the top and reduces water pressure to a minimum, the rod is not strained by the casting.

Depth fascinates. Having a fly line deep down in a spring pool for instance, places great emphasis on the 'telegraphic' sensations we get through our fingertips. On cold days when the fingers have turned numb I have discovered just now important this fingertip sense is in deep line fishing. The pull of a salmon when the fingertips are numb is felt in your arms through the rod, and while it is still a thrilling enough matter, the touch of the fingers on the line makes the take so much better felt, so much more sensitive a thing, that it is a higher experience altogether.

CHAPTER FIVE

The Pursuit of Depth: (2) Spinning

To the inexperienced angler there seems to be no problem in getting a spinning bait to sink, yet the expert, fishing deeply for salmon in spring waters, in cold flood water or in late season fishing finds the problem of proper sinking his constant preoccupation. Most of the changes in bait design that I have seen over the past few years are connected with deep fishing and I would like to review some of these here, throwing light on the techniques of salmon spinning they are designed to support.

The common-sense way to achieve depth in spinning is to add weight to the terminal tackle. That can mean one of two things; adding weight to the trace, above the bait, or increasing the weight of the lure itself. Adding weight to the trace is the traditional way of doing this. I have in my spinning kit a number of leads designed to carry out this. The one I favour most is the spiral lead, which consists of a tapered cylinder of lead mounted on wire provided with a spiral groove running its full length. A spiral of brass wire protrudes from the lead at each end. To mount this lead the line is merely twisted round the spiral groove and fed into the brass wire. The brass wire may be pinched together for maximum security, although I have never found this necessary. An added use of the spiral lead is that it can be bent into a shallow crescent after mounting to provide a first class anti-kink device.

The faults with this best known of leads are those of most other trace weights; they make casting poor and they cause a 'bolas' effect in the casting which can often cause snagging with the trace. Once in the water they fish well and have one very important advantage. Since the spiral lead is virtually snag free by its shape you can let it bump the stones of the bottom of the salmon stream while your lighter bait, say a wooden devon, rises and falls in the current a few inches above the bottom. On the Spey this is the acknowledged method of fishing the rocky, highly productive lies of the middle river.

Other types of trace weight include simple devices like the lead washer bent over the trace, the large pierced bullet threaded on to the cast, and the various designs of more elaborate leads suspended in various ways from the swivels of the trace or the trace itself. In terms of mere sinking, all work. Many, however, are fiddly to attach and worse, some are distinctly hard to remove or replace with cold hands. All share the faults of 'bolas' casting effects, but all share the merits of keeping the trace well down in the water while allowing a lighter bait to fish flexibly in the varying stream.

A second and equally obvious way of sinking baits is to make the baits themselves heavy. On Tay where a great deal of heavy spinning is done in the early months of the year I have recently seen two local designs of heavy devon. The first of these was a wooden devon with a lead nose. This was made by a most craftsmanlike process in which the minnow began life as a block of wood which was drilled out and had a copper tube pressed into its core. It was then turned down to the right size but, instead of finishing off the nose the minnow was left with about a quarter of its length stripped to the tube. On to this a lead nose was cast in a little mould like a thimble. The whole minnow was then turned down to its final proportions, fins were fitted in the wooden part and the final bait was painted.

This produces a bait which some have jocularly said comes in three weights, Heavy, Extra Heavy and Damned Heavy! In fishing it is claimed that the weight forward is counteracted by the pull of the line and the effect is a straight swimming bait. Experiments have been made with fin angle to give more or less lift to make the heavy bait take up certain angles in fishing, say for slow water, thin streamy water, etc. I feel that this is an unbalanced bait which would only fish properly in certain set conditions of stream. The bait takes salmon very readily in spring and casts phenomenal distances with a large sea-type fixed spool reel and heavy monofilament.

A more refined devon produced on the banks of the Tay is the minnow with the lead belt. This is a painstakingly designed and produced wooden bait which goes through all the usual production processes but has a groove chiselled out of its cylinder at its point of balance. This is filled with molten lead and the finished shape is turned down to the required proportions. The fins are set in the lead in this case. This minnow spins deeply and on an even keel. In gentler water it bumps the bottom, but remains fishing on an even keel. On some of the fatter beats of Tay this is a standard bait with hundreds of salmon to its credit.

The other, less obvious way of attaining depth is by the use of a diving vane on the bait. This takes one from the realm of minnows into the kingdom of plugs. The most famous of the Tay plugs is the Kynoch Killer, a plastic cone-shaped bait with a protruding lower jaw which acts as a most efficient diving vane. Another is the Lucky Lou, an American plug. Yet another is the Finnish Rapala. All of these baits are light and if no movement is brought to bear on them by fishing them into the stream in such a way that they bite down into the water, they will float. This can be a godsend if one is fishing really nasty snag-ridden water. I have fished the Rapala for instance from a boat when devons would have snagged every cast. It was possible to use the floating characteristics to lift the bait over the boulders but to use the diving vane by pulling sharply on the line to take the bait down to the fishing lies.

Recently some attempt has been made with such designs as the Ajax devon to combine a diving vane with a fairly heavy devon. I have only just started fishing this design and can only say that it swims well and dives well and may prove to be a good deep bait.

Depth is of such vital importance to a salmon fisher that he is willing to spend considerable time and money experimenting. I recommend to handymen the designs I have described, some of which can be bought locally in Perth and elsewhere, but which might be made in a home workshop without too much trouble. From my own fishing point of view I incline to the lead-belted minnow rather than the lead-headed minnow. But anything which got one away from the swinging 'bolas' of the lead-up-the-trace technique I have fished for years is welcome. Yet for really careful fishing of rocky lies (often wildly pro-ductive lies) the light wooden devon with some form of trace lead is the only answer, if there is not a boat on the beat.

CHAPTER SIX

A Case for Early Spring Fly Fishing

Spinning for salmon on the Tay in early spring is usually carried out with something like a religious conviction that it is the only reasonable way to try to tempt spring run fish. Where the beat has a boat on its pools spinning baits like devons, or wobbling baits like spoons or plugs are 'harled' over the lies in a way that exploits the slow, deep hanging bait in an effective way. To arrive at a main Tay beat in January, February or March and announce that one intended to fly fish for springers would sometimes amount to a ghillie's joke. Yet, on my regular Tay beat last spring (1968) each day we have fished we have spent several hours with fly and the results have not only been encouraging in terms of fish caught, but in terms of understanding our pools better and the ways of the springers in them, the results have made us think twice about the conventions of the Tay.

On our first day out in January 1968, in a water running at 4 ft. 6 in. on the gauge, one of my guests, fishing fly, killed the first springer of the year. The fish was not taken from a spring lie, but from a lie beside fast water where the main stream of the pool rushes down in a narrow neck over shingle and forms our main holding pool. We killed autumn fish and summer fish in previous seasons on fly in this water, and in the autumn of 1967 in a six foot flood we had eleven fish from this stream, giving us our best day for the season. So it was a lie known to us and well fished in warmer waters later in the season, but it was not counted a spring lie. One of the local ghillies, who has known this pool for forty years, insisted that fish were never taken from this stream 'in the old days' until June and he firmly held that it would be a waste of time fishing it before that date. I remember taking a small April fish on a spoon in that stream one season and finding him unrepentant, although interested that there should be a 'daft one' there. The ghillie's view, which was shared by other anglers fishing the beat, was that a spring lie had to be slow, deep and 'holding' (that great intangible quality), with just enough current to make the bait work well over the salmon. Returns seem to bear him out until one reflects that anglers seldom fish elsewhere on the grounds that 'it would be a waste of good fishing time'. Circularity reigns. We have broken out and have started fly fishing in spring for two reasons. Firstly we like fishing the fly, even with sinking lines on our rods; secondly, we are trying to exploit to the full specialised fly fishing tackle (like sinking lines) which has come into prominence in the last decade and calls many of our established fishing practices into question.

The water the first springer came from was no more than three feet deep and in character it is streamy with spits or underwater ridges of gravel running out into the faster water at an acute angle to the left bank. These angled spits—a common feature of shingly salmon pools where there is a high scouring action in a heavy stream—make small changes of direction of the marginal water and these small sub streams mark salmon lies as surely as arrows on the surface of the stream would. At this time of year most of these lies are occupied by kelts and they come readily to the fly (far more readily than they come to the spinner in shallow water) with the result that one's fly rod is usually bent into some kind of take at intervals during the fly fishing period of the day. It was after a series of rather interesting encounters with kelts on fly here (one ran five times up the fast water!) that the first springer took. It practically swallowed a Waddington 2/o Yellow Dog and fought strongly in the fast water before being tailed out.

Two weeks elapsed before my day on the beat came up again. The water was lower, running at 2 ft. 6 in. on the gauge, and we began the day when a well shaped fourteen pounder took my black and gold toby on the third cast in one of the recognised spring lies. Nothing else happened all forenoon, but after lunch I crossed over to the left bank with my guest and we began our period of 'compulsory' fly fishing. Water temperature was

36 deg. F. and the day had grown milder as the sun broke through after a frosty misty morning. I took my guest to the main stream, showed him the square yard of water where the first fly-caught springer had come from and left him to fish down with a Wet Cel No. 11 on his fifteen foot rod, and a two inch Yellow Dog tube which his young son had tied up for him. I began some way further down the stream and as I waded in (and one must wade carefully when fish are in two to three feet of water) I saw a quick movement in the very part of the stream above me that my guest was beginning to fish. He was into a fish in a few casts, a splendid fifteen pounder with sea lice on it —one of these Tay springers that for shape and sheen take the breath away. Our uncharacteristic spring lie, and our fly rods, had scored another success.

At that point in February the beat had produced (on our days only) four fish in three days fishing, two of which had been taken on fly. By the end of February, after three weeks of cold low water when neither bait nor fly was effective, we had accounted for six fish, four on bait, two on fly. These are not figures of any statistical significance, of course. In terms of our own records over the last four seasons on this pool, this is the best opening burst we have had, and as far as we can judge, this is the first time fly has been fished consistently in any spring, probably since the advent of good spinning tackle in the post war years.

What we are saying to ourselves and to our guests about spring fly fishing is this. If you don't fly fish, you won't know whether it is a useful spring method or not. Our early brace point to fly fishing the thinner water beside the streams as 'bonus' water – that is, water where a running fish might pause for a breather, or where single fish might be in shallow lies. We are also pressing the pleasures of fly fishing as a relief from the usual steady bank spinning we see done on the pools. It is like a selling operation! Yet at least two rods went home with a fresh fish as a result.

It is a commonplace to note that the sinking fly line and the large tube fly, Waddington or Drury have overcome many of the difficulties of sunk fly fishing from the days of the No. 6 or 7 silk line and the very large 'meat hook' singles or gravel-dredging doubles of spring flies. We can now fish with the line deep, the fly large, but the lure itself not bottom seeking. I think a wading angler needs a fly that (like a wooden devon with a lead up the trace) fishes up a little from the bottom. On deep pools like the Junction Pool on Tweed at Kelso, where the angler is casting from a boat, the leaded tube fly is usual. It works well. We had an excellent day with this heavy line, heavy fly technique there in the second week of February this year. But casting with a deep line and a heavy fly can be somewhat specialised. The double roll downstream that is often necessary before the cast proper can be made irks many fly fishers. With a lighter fly and a reasonable stream to work for you a single downstream roll will pluck the fly from the depths and allow a spey cast or an overhead to follow without much fuss. This rolling, speying and overheading demands a really competent rod and I cannot praise my Sharpe's fourteen foot impregnated fly rod enough for the way it performs. Spliced greenheart rods are often used for this work by ghillies, particularly on the Spey, but I have found these great rods rather too heavy for me in sheer terms of avoirdupois.

On the Spey last year, fishing fly after the main fishing of the day was over (we came down after an early dinner) we killed fresh fish on large single 1/0 flies. These were the first fish of the spring on fly, but they were fish taken on a floating line, very much in the early season floating line style suggested by Wood. Would not the Spey yield fish well to modern sunk line tactics much earlier than this? I have no figures to go on in this, but my impression is that few anglers even mount a fly rod until late March or early April and then they fish with a floater – often quite successfully with water temperatures in the lower forties and even better.

If it is an illusion that salmon fight much better on fly than on spinning tackle, it is a compelling one. My own experience is that fish run farther on fly, leap more and make upstream more. On spinner I seem often to be running downstream after fish which doggedly take line. The reluctance with which we *give* line in spinning may have a lot to do with this. A slipping clutch on a fixed spool reel, or a drag restricted multiplier drum may seem to be giving the fish line at a merry rate, but in fact the fish is working far harder for its line than against a fly reel check. Above all, the sinuous long rod, satisfyingly bent into a salmon, gives one a tremendous feeling of the way a fish is pulsating in the fight, and this is at once a more thrilling aspect of the fight and a key to the stage of fatigue of the salmon. These features are often almost completely absent from the bait rod fight.

There is little doubt in our minds as we fish the Tay that, the more we study our pools and streams, the more we want to fly fish them; the more we fly fish them intelligently (and luckily) the more we learn and the more we enjoy our fishing. Conventions of spinning, and worse, of harling, often make tenant somewhat incurious, somewhat given to uncritical habits of fishing, and somewhat less productive than they might otherwise be.

CHAPTER SEVEN

A 'Gee' on the Thurso

In terms of the volume of its water or the length of its water-course, the Thurso River is hardly one of the leading rivers of Scotland, but in terms of its salmon fishing I doubt whether it has many equals in the country. It is only twenty five miles from the locks at Lochmore in the heather moors of Caithness to the town of Thurso where the river flows over the weirs and into the waters of the Pentland Firth. Between Lochmore and the sea lie fifteen salmon fishing beats varied from fast rocky stretches of water like beat twelve to gentle streamy beats like beat five at the town of Halkirk and slow moorland pools on what some anglers call the 'dead waters' of beat eight and elsewhere. For me no part of the Thurso is 'dead'; quite the opposite. One glimpse of its waters and its promise of sport makes my pulse beat faster.

In April 1965 I made my third visit to the Thurso and during my stay I was lucky enough to be asked by the tenant of the rotation of upper beats to fish his water with him one afternoon in the week before Easter. My own beat that day should have been No. 5, but a sudden spate made it unfishable and I was delighted to try one of the high beats of the fishing.

Beat fifteen runs from the fish pass at Lochmore down to Loch Beg, a first class resting place for early salmon waiting to ascend into the loch above. I was lucky enough to strike the beat on a day when there was enough rain to bring the fish up from Loch Beg but hardly enough to let them run the fishpass freely. There was in the stretch a good stock of very fresh fish, typical small Thurso springers – high in the shoulder and shining clean with that bluish sheen tingeing the flanks and deepening over the back. Water and stock were on our side, but

49

weather was not. A fierce wind was tearing overhead and during the day rain, hail and snow fell in short piercingly cold showers.

How do you tackle salmon in cold semi-winter conditions like that? I had with me what I consider to be the ideal tackle for the job. I had my Sharpe's fourteen foot spliced cane fly rod – as sweet a fourteen footer as you will ever wield – and I had on my reel one of the first 'speycaster' wet cel lines which Farlow's produced. The idea of a 'speycaster' is to provide a modified weight forward line which has enough belly to be rolled or speycast before the shooting line in the hand is taken out. On my prototype there was eighteen yards in the taper and the belly which made nearly perfect rolling weight for my rod. With the wind, overhead casting was out of the question, or very hazardous indeed.

With a heavy fly line like the AFTM 10 wet cel you do not need to cast a heavy fly. In fact, to use a heavy fly is to court snagging on a frustrating scale. I use a light, but large tube, a Garry Dog tied on polythene, an inch and a half long. This fishes deeply, but rises up off the bottom rather than fishes down on to the bottom. The deeply fished line and light fly however have their own difficulties. One is that salmon takes may be followed by a tremendous rush on the part of the fish and with a heavy line well drowned you can lose fish. This happened once during the day. Compensation for this hazard is found in the solid way deep salmon take. When you feel the pull it is the fish turning away with the fly and that usually means hooking the fish well back in the angle of the jaw.

The first fish of the afternoon was one I saw moving in the tail of the bridge pool. I covered it with no result, then fishing over it again but mending the line to give it a chance to sink further before the current seized it, I succeeded in presenting the fish with a deep, slow fly which it took at once. It was a fast little fish, only seven pounds in weight, but proportionately magnificent and in splendid spring sheen.

The top beat of Thurso has several slowish rushy stretches not far below the bridge and one of these the weedy pool is a favourite cast of mine. A bank of rushes forms an island in the river and below it salmon lie deeply in a lie just out of the main current of the river. To fish a fly deeply over a lie like this with a distance of about eighteen yards between your stance on the left bank and the tail of the reed bed is a tricky problem. The fly can so easily reach the lie and be drawn off course by the main current and in this way may fail to present itself to the salmon in a steady, deep way. I used the shooting line of the 'speycaster' to help me out of this difficulty. By overcasting by a couple of yards and throwing a loop of line upstream to counteract the current, the fly and the heavy line was allowed to sink. Then the line was retrieved by hand until the fly was felt to be fishing and the current was used to swing the fly steadily and a good depth over the lie. Twice I snagged on the reeds, but managed to draw the fly clear. Then it went down as I planned. There was a slight tremor and a pull and I hooked salmon No. 2 of the afternoon. This was a fish of the twelve pound class and its first reaction was to leap twice and run hard against the sunk line. This seemed to tear the hook hold and although I held on to the fish for a minute or so, it persistently leaped and finally threw the hook. I suspect it was hooked too far forward in the mouth anyway from the way it behaved.

The bridge pool again yielded a nice eight pounder and again the fly was taken practically off the river bottom. I was beginning to feel that unforgettable glow of having had splendid luck when I reeled up and went on to the bridge as the day wore on towards its close. A local man met me there and described a fantastic piece of fishing he had had by dapping late in the evening for the salmon which rose, mad, like spring trout, in the eddies and streams of the pool below. He said, 'They took the gee', and he described the mad, whimlike behaviour of the fish as they rose to a fly dapped and dragged on the surface. It was, I recognised, a kind of 'dibbling' technique not unlike Helmsdale fishing and I managed to get my chosen fly, No. 1 bushily-tied Garry Dog, cutting the surface on a dropper.

I was fascinated to see a salmon glide from the depths and miss my fly completely. Two casts later it came again and this time I watched it open its mouth, take in the fly and turn back down for the depths. I tightened and was into him and after a hard fight he came into the eddy above the bridge where I was able to tail him. Ten pounds, and covered with sea lice.

I called it a day and packed the salmon in a large straw bass,

Fish were still occasionally showing in the bridge pool, but the day was clearly over. It still blew hard from the Northwest and a cold steely evening sky promised winter instead of spring. For me this was a day of magnificent fishing, on a river I had yearned to fish as a boy fifteen years before. It was hardly a big bag in terms of the Thurso's fabulous successes, but it was a day of wind and weather defied and of the victory of tackle and tactics over conditions. Most memorable of all were the fish, shining fresh, hard fighting, and looking like prototypes of salmon for the original patterns of creation.

The words the local man had used rang in my ears however. The fish, he said, had 'taken the gee'. It was a word I had never heard before. Clearly he took it to mean mad and unpredictable behaviour in the context of salmon suddenly going crazy and rising freely on a cold April evening. I went to my Jamieson when I got back to Edinburgh (Jamieson's Etymological Dictionary of the Scottish Language, 1808) and found the word listed. There, it was given the meaning 'to become pettish and unmanageable' and the contexts cited were almost all about the unpredictable behaviour of women. A wife waiting for a husband was said to 'take the gee' and in a popular song lads were advised not to let the *gees* of the lassies worry them.

Other uses of the word come nearer the Thurso. For example, poets are said to be given to taking *gees* when they are not well guided.

'Ye know ill gyding gerders mony *gees*,
And specially in poets for example.'

Montgomerie.

Sulky women, fickle girls and poets . . . but the word was used on the bridge of beat fifteen of the Thurso to describe the behaviour of salmon! I now have a very meaningful personal context for the term. To me 'gee' is more than unpredictable, more than whim; it contains a grain of the miraculous. To see salmon go wild like that is contest enough for any word. I hope this madness comes my way again.

CHAPTER EIGHT

The View from the Bridge

In my bait box, beside the conventional wooden devons, the slotless metal devons (hardly ever used) and the odd plug bait lie three Finnish lures called *Rapalas*. One of them is an original, bought in Helsinki in 1959 for catching big trout in Lapland. The others are from several I obtained in Farlow's in London, after they began importing Rapalas from Finland. To look at, they are almost too perfect. They are baits formed of moulded foam plastic and shaped like thin, elegant sprats, and in their colour they grade perfectly naturally from a scaly silver to a pure white on the belly. Almost at once an angler might condemn these baits for being ridiculously detailed for a bait intended to be impressionistic in use.

One spring recently, fishing the River Teviot I arrived to find a medium-full river flowing greenish clear and cold – ideal conditions for bait fishing. In addition, there were reports of numbers of small springers in the eight pound class being taken from the water. I fished as my tradition dictated and presented wooden devons to the likely lies, but by five in the afternoon, as the spring day was waning, I had caught nothing. With the edge off my enthusiasm I began fiddling about the less likely and less used baits of my tackle box and for fun decided to use an old bridge which spanned the river as a vantage point from which I could watch the action of the bait I was trying as it fished in towards me. To make this an even more interesting experiment, the shingly run below the bridge was a redd of the previous winter and several kelt sea trout and two or three big grayling were lounging on the gravel.

The first bait I tried was a plastic devon and it whirled through the water like a torpedo and, first cast, scattered the

53

sea trout and the grayling as it passed. 'No good', I thought, and took out my box to try another. The Rapalas caught my eye and choosing a two-and-a-half inch one, I attached it to my salmon spinning tackle. It was so light, being a foam plastic bait, a floating-diving plug impelled down by a vane under its head, that I had to add lead to the trace to give it weight to be cast. Out it sailed, making a flat parabola from the old bridge and falling with a 'splat' on the water some thirty yards down the long run. It fished in a fascinating way, shivering and fluttering in the stream and as I reeled in, it would dive down, to stop, turn in the stream and surface again when I ceased reeling in. Then a sea trout sped over to it and swirled at it. Another followed and held its nose against the tail of my bait for several yards. A grayling left its lie and swung, dorsal fin up, towards the bait, obviously interested. No fish took, but every fish the Rapala passed showed interest. What excellent observing conditions I had from the bridge!

I cast again, further this time and I sent the bait far down the stream to where it slowed up somewhat and formed a small pothole. The Rapala went down and I saw it flashing away in the green water. There was suddenly a magnificent, momentary picture in the green transparency of a long silver side sliding in an arc at the bait and appreciably later I felt the line tighten and the rod dip as the fish turned away and hooked itself well. This was no grayling, nor spent sea trout. This was a salmon, and by the look of it a fresh one. From my perch on the old bridge I watched the fish run fast up the stream, turn back again, lunge on the surface and speed back down again to the lie from which it took. My fishing friend arrived, and two other local men, and from the bridge as a natural gallery one angler and three spectators watched the clear fight of a clean salmon below them.

It soon became clear that I must get down to the river and somehow tail this fish out. But the sides of the bridge were twelve feet high and awkward trees prevented my lengthening line and going the long way round to the river bank, by leaving the bridge altogether. This is where the spectators became part of an angling team. First I handed over the rod to my friend and he fought the fish while I 'dreeped' the twelve foot wall and landed in a heap on the grassy bank below. Then the rod was handed down, butt first, and the pick-up of the multiplier left off lest the fish should run during the critical moment of transfer. I grasped the rod, reeled in fast and watched the line gathered up, then pause, tighten and move. He was still on!

The easy bit came next. My friend came clattering down the wall behind me, took off his tailer and inside a minute had the fish on the bank. It was an eight-and-a-half-pound springer in superb shape, glistening in all its bluish and pinkish undertones. Rapala had scored.

A few days after this encounter, in a short visit to the Spey at Aberlour, during which the Rapala again proved itself and took a fifteen pounder from the 'Creepie' pool, I was first the spectator, then the collaborator in tailing a fresh ten pounder hooked from a bridge. And oddly enough that too began as a kind of dabble. The angler had seen a revolver lying in the bottom of the Spey and keen to find out more about it – to find out whether it was a toy or the real thing, he tried to snag it with his wooden devon. As the devon fluttered and dangled a salmon hitherto unnoticed emerged and took and after some trouble was brought in to a place where my tailer could be used.

Both bridge experiences tell something of the same tale. The bait fished on the 'hang' below the angler – just as a boat-fished bait might be – is a deadly one for salmon. Harling owes part of its success to this hanging technique. Of course harling also has a mobile platform from which lies are searched thoroughly and each lie is presented with a hanging bait, fluttering above the salmon. Further the boat-harled bait has the advantage of yet another very attractive feature of bait (or fly) presentation – the lure which is swinging off the salmon lie after dangling there for a second or two. Salmon seem to be keen, sometimes, to snatch at a bait that they have refused when it was presented 'on a plate'. There is, of course a human characteristic very like this, which we all know. It is often easier to sell the 'last one' which is being taken out of the window because an old customer has asked for it to be reserved!

I have fly fished from bridges too, principally on the Thurso on two pools – the top pool of Beat 15, and the high bridge over the Long Pool of Beat 12. In the case of the top pool it is a double bonus for not only is there a splendid apron of the pool below the bridge where springers lie and where one can always be sure of stock, but above the bridge there is a great eddy under the fish pass to Loch More and it it possible to fish this as a productive reserve pool from the same bridge. In Chapter 7 we describe one of the excellent results of this bridge fishing, for, with the tremendous advantage of height over the lies, one can drag a fly very well through the surface and fish a dropper to perfection.

Apart from the obvious hazards of the fish going through the bridge and smashing you, there are distinct advantages in playing a fish from above. The runs seem so much less of a strain on the tackle, mainly because one is able to keep so much line out of the water and avoid the dreadful drowned-line drag which so often results in a break. Simple geometry also tells us that a running fish played from a height above, has to go much further to take line. Indeed, I sometimes wonder whether fish played from the high casting platforms of some of our Highland rivers, say the Ross-shire (Bonar Bridge) Carron at Glencalvie, would not be rather dull fish to handle, for the height above them would take away all the powerful running character of the fight.

Bridges are, of course, on some stretches, taboo, and one should always be quite sure about local conventions before fishing from one. In most cases I would avoid them unless there was an active tradition of having a cast from one. Nevertheless, where a bridge cast is available, it can often be very entertaining, if only from the point of view that you can see what the fly is doing and how the fish are reacting.

CHAPTER NINE

Hanging a Fly on the Tay

This is the story of two days on the Tay; two days on the same beat in summer. One of the days, the first, had an ideal water running, but we only managed to take one fish for two rods. The following week, in very low water conditions, we applied one of the lessons we had learned from our previous visit and we had a bumper day.

The first day was a success story of a rather specialised kind. It was the first day we had managed to take a salmon on fly from our beat this summer. The middle Tay fishes oddly to the fly, I find. Fish showing in lies sometimes boil at your flies, but it is only when dead low water conditions come that we have any real record of success in takes. This impression I have of the Tay being a rather unresponsive river for fly fishing may relate to the fact that most anglers spin the Tay or harl it from boats and the fly never really gets any documented success, or it may result from my own faulty techniques, in fishing the Tay. It is, after all, a bigger water, deeper in its runs and main lies, harder in its races and in its wading than most other waters. This alone makes my two seasons of continual fishing of one beat hardly long enough to decide about long term fly fishing chances.

The first of the two days saw two of us armed with fly rods and spinners. The water was around nine inches above dead low summer conditions, according to the gauge and things looked in nice ply for fly fishing. I had not managed to raise one fish to the fly by eleven o'clock and I decided to try spinning. My guest, from the Nith, thought he had never seen such a lovely piece of fly water and promptly raised and hooked a nice little fish of seven-and-a-half-pounds in one of the main lies that I had just fished a bait through. Then, hearing about some fast water above the island, he tramped off. I was to follow.

I arrived up at the faster water to find my companion in a great state of excitement. He had raised two fish, hooked a third and had lost it within a few seconds. As I watched him fish down the fast water again he raised one and missed it then raised and hooked another salmon. This fish came unstuck in a few seconds. It was a batch of very promising activity, but a very frustrating experience. Moving all these salmon, and not grassing a fish was rather daunting.

We talked about it and decided that speed and depth of water was the trouble. There the Tay is hard to wade because of a powerful, steady current which can roll boulders as big as footballs. Sometimes one's foot lifts a good sized stone there and the force takes the stone several yards down with it before it manages to find an anchor on the shingle and boulders of the bed. In such fast water, with broken water below, the fly tends to come off the fish very quickly indeed, and it is tempting for the angler to wade not much further than a good knee-deep in view of the force of the glide. Thus the line is often thrown far too squarely over the lies and salmon keen on the fly, moving to it, miss it.

The following week the sun shone relentlessly and the Tay fell fast to its 'bare bones' level. On our next allocated day on the beat the water was below the bottom of the gauge. The pools *looked* the same, but the very fast water we had had such difficulty with was much more wadable. With belly waders and well studded brogues I was able to get well out over the fast glide. The fly could thus be moved reasonably slowly, with a good bit of line control, and fish should manage to take it.

I chose a No. 6 double shrimp to get a little weight in the fly and to prevent it skating. I had my first take very shortly after edging my way out into the fast water and throwing a long line down to the lie. It was a full-blooded take, well engulfed and well hooked. That part of it was fine, but I was well out in a fast glide, leaning against tons of Tay water, and my fish was thirty yards below me and was now off downstream, running hard with the water and heading for the very turbulent stream below.

It takes an interminable time to stumble out of a river when half your faculties are intent on playing a salmon. But it was a relief to feel the shingle dry under one's feet and to clatter down it as hard as one could go in belly waders and brogues. There really ought to be a prize race for anglers in waders. I'm in perpetual training; I always seem to be clattering down the bank with a fish, or to help someone land a fish.

This salmon took over seventy yards of line off before doubling back upstream, drowning my line and more or less regaining its lie. I was lucky to get my line back safely and get on to proper terms with the fish for the fast water had taken its wind away, as the running had mine. It came in reasonably easily after that, fifteen pounds, with sea lice, shaped as a Tay fish usually is – high, short, deep. Perfect.

This success was repeated within ten minutes, with a fourteen pounder on the same fly from the same lie. It was purely a question of presentation. While one could reach a lie from all sorts of different points, one could only fish it properly from a desperate wade with a long line. Anyone looking at me fishing that lie would have been forgiven for thinking me rather extreme. What could be gained by such wading and such exhausting casting? But the rule is simply this; covering a lie is not enough; the fly must cross it at a speed which will alow the slow salmon time to move up, engulf it and turn away.

Both salmon were hooked with both points of the double, well embedded about three quarters way between the snout and the angle of the jaw. This in itself shows that, given even more time to turn the fish would have taken the fly further back still and have been hooked in the angle itself. I struck neither fish. I let the salmon pull the hook home itself against the weight of water on the line. Indeed, had the rod top not been held very high, giving the salmon plenty of slack to take with them, one of these fish would have broken me for sure on the take. Its first pull on the take was severe enough to make a gathering belly of line on the surface of the glide skip off the top and dart inwards. Had I 'struck' I should have had the rod top pulled right down, with maximum tension falling on the line and a break for certain resulting.

We finished the day with four fish, not all taken on fly, but all from within ten yards or so of the place my brace on the fly came from. All were fresh and the biggest which took a small wooden devon, was eighteen pounds. The spinning line did not drown so readily and the fish was under far less water pressure, but we also noticed that the fish on the spinning rod fought far less well than those on the fly rod. There were no long, singing runs, no great lunges and sudden changes of direction. Something about the fly rod brings the most sporting side of a salmon to the top. I catch a good number of salmon on spinning gear, and I am thrilled by it, but a fly well hung is like an arrow well shot, and a salmon take on the fly is so much more of an experience than the sullen pull to the spinning bait that it seems to be from another range of fishing altogether. This is why I have been given to muttering recently a complaint along these lines – If only the Tay would yield fish to the fly more often, what an unparalleled water it would be. Well, perhaps we have learned one of its secrets, and it will.

CHAPTER TEN

Learning from Marginal Salmon

Most salmon fishers are well aware of the stages their fishing goes through in the course of a season. They expect a period of bait fishing or heavy fly fishing in spring, they know they will change when the weather becomes warmer to lighter sunk tackle and to greased line tackle, and at the end of summer they again change over to heavier rods, lines and flies. What fascinates me are the marginal cases when tackle not typical of the conditions takes fish and one is shocked into seeing how stylised our salmon fishing techniques have become.

I claim I was bullied into ruining a day on Tweed one October – and it may serve to show how easy it is to think in a stylised fashion about salmon, and lose sport as a result. I accepted the local dictum on Tweed that autumn fish like deeply sunk baits and in October I spent a day trying to sink my flies well. My rod was a fourteen footer, my line a Wet Cel AFTM. 10 and my fly a large tube, built up of sections; my leader was of 16 lb. b.s. I did nothing at all in three hours' fishing, but I did meet a novice fisher who had a soft twelve foot glass rod, a ridiculously light silk line (No. 2 silk) and he was fishing a tube fly about three-quarters of an inch long – a Yellow Dog which he had tied up himself in his hotel the previous night. He followed me through a pool and hooked a fish, unfortunately losing it after a few minutes' fight. 'A fluke,' I thought, 'This is the autumn'.

I fished on, mending and sinking my heavy line and the novice, after a chat with me, in which ironically he asked my advice on all kinds of problems, moved down to the next pool. Quarter of an hour later I was disturbed by a lorry driver stumbling excitedly up the bank to inform me that the young chap was fast into a fish and the road was jammed with parked cars watching the spectacle. No one had the knowledge to help him land it. Would I come at once?

The rest of the story is plain. I tailed out a magnificent sixteen pounder which had taken the little Yellow Dog and before the day was over he had moved another fish and killed a good sea trout. A light line, a small fly and success, in October after the frosts had come. One case does not prove a theory, but when it is a marginal case it makes one think about one's own policies.

It made me think back to a previous autumn and to a previous spring when, on different waters, when others had fished traditional deep fly tackle, a small fly and a floating line had taken salmon on Spey. The conditions were hard frost, a falling water and all anglers in the area spinning. Some salmon, I should say, fell to spinners at the same time. Then a local angler began greased lining, took a good sea trout, then took one salmon and ran another. I checked the water temperature – 38 deg. F. The air was at that moment around forty. It was a marginal case, and it provided some much more pleasant sport on a fly rod for one man, than bait tackle could ever have given. Standing watching the spectacle with my heavy bait I felt annoyed with my own stylised thinking on the sport.

When April comes the month of marginal tactics is confirmed. For future April fishing I have made a resolution – I shall always, during the month, err on the light side and try to get myself out of this awful deep-and-heavy spring rut. I firmly expect to find that from the margins between traditional deep fishing and traditional greased line conditions I shall learn something radical about salmon. Perhaps April and October are the two months in which an intelligent exploitation of marginal conditions will succeed. They are the boundaries of winter.

It may seem improbable, but ought we not to extend our theory of margins to spates too? They, also, are the 'boundaries of winter', figuratively. Spates can lower water temperature suddenly and dramatically and a thundery shower of hail on a summer day can chill the air well below the water temperature.

I discovered one September when fishing the Earn that I was

the only person taking fish on a certain stretch. I had three fish in two days and I moved several more. I was fishing summer tackle – a thirteen foot greased line rod, an eight pound leader and a light No. 2 Hairy Mary on a low water iron. The line was the vital part of my tackle however. It was a trial of a quick-sinking terylene line, and I had merely run it on to my fly reel in place of the floater I normally fished greased line with. The line sank well in the fresh running water I found after a small late summer spate. I found by experimenting, that by mending and throwing off extra line, I could sink the light fly well in the long hard glide leading into a good pool. I took a grilse from the glide, and in the pool itself hooked and lost a much heavier fish. I also killed on the small deeply fished hairwing a heavy red cock salmon of eighteen pounds. This was marginal fishing since it was technically too early to fish deeply with heavy lines and flies, yet in that spate it was cold enough to warrant it.

Rather than try to peg the theory I have to temperatures and to water heights I prefer to make for myself a principle of behaviour. In the marginal cases I mention success came to the man fishing in a mode untypical of the time of year. Yet in each case there was something to recommend it. In each case the tackle was lighter than one might have argued was dictated by the spring or the autumn or the spate. In one case the lighter tackle was deeply sunk, in the others, while other anglers fished heavy, deeply sunk flies, the little fly nearer the surface scored. If I use the principle of fishing lighter than the conditions seem to suggest in a marginal situation, I shall not only fish in an aesthetically more pleasant way, I shall have a good chance of fishing in a more successful mode, and perhaps I shall learn more about my fish in the marginal conditions of the season.

CHAPTER ELEVEN

Fishing 'Dead' Waters

On the middle and upper reaches of many Scottish salmon rivers there are slow-flowing moorland stretches of river rather like natural canals, which have come to be known by anglers as 'dead waters'. This is one of the worst descriptive titles in fishing. Many must take it that dead waters yield no fish, or are dour and uninteresting to fish. My contention is that I am an angler and nothing in the world of game fishing waters fails to interest me. Yet it is true that without a few wrinkles about the slower reaches of rivers some people might get a bad impression of water which would yield them good sport.

In the first place, dead waters are not what they look. The waters of the middle Thurso for example are not without flow as they might appear to a superficial glance. They are areas of good stream, but the depth of the channel and the configuration of the banks means that the flow is very even. If you fish a deep fly in spring on say beat eight of the Thurso you will soon realise that there is need for mending after the cast to keep the angle of presentation right and even a big fly in a cold water will find enough current to fish. If you feel that your fly is not fishing up off the lies in an attractive manner in deep fly work a very good idea is to let the line do the sinking and fish a lighter tube fly to use to the maximum the effect of the stream. I have had excellent sport on the Thurso in spring using a Wet Cel line and an inch and a half Garry Dog tied on a polythene tube. The line took the fly down, but the fly fished up in the current. To adopt the technique of fishing a heavy fly and making it take the line down is, to my mind, making the fly swim less well, especially in slower currents.

On the River Earn in Perthshire where the middle and lower

Above: Mr Hugh Stewart fly fishing the streamy water above the Sauce Pool on beat twelve of the Thurso river, Caithness. *Below:* Ashore for lunch on a spit in Loch Eilt, Inverness-shire. This famous sea trout loch is noted for its dapping and sea trout up to 18 lb. in weight have been taken in recent years. Mr Alistair Murray, the fishing tenant, is on the left

Drifting Loch Maree, trying for a trout or a sea trout. Kinlochewe water

reaches of the river are inclined to be 'dead' there is a considerable problem in fishing the lies properly since the deadness is, like the Thurso, an evenness of flow, not a slackness. Wading the Earn reminds you of the power of steadily moving water. Trying to mend your line properly to allow your fly to fish down to autumn fish lies twenty yards out is a task which many salmon fly fishers have found beyond their powers.

Most fishers wait for a wind to ruffle the surface of the dead waters before expecting fish to take. There is no doubt at all that a wind helps greatly, particularly in summer fishing. I personally like a downstream wind because it helps me to make long down and across casts and if a fish offers as soon as the fly lands it helps me to have a straight cast for the take and to be in a position to get into contact with the fish without fighting an upstream belly.

I was very frustrated one day when I was fishing for sea trout on a large flat on the Sheil. Try as I might, accelerating the cast viciously and punching a narrow loop hard into the upstream wind, I could not prevent my leader doubling back on the line just as the loop unrolled on the water. The line beat the wind, but the flies failed to. After two takes by sea trout as the cast flicked past them on landing – takes I could do nothing with because of a wind belly upstream – I gave up and travelled a mile upstream to where the river looped and using the wind downstream, landed one fish and lost another in a short stretch of water.

Dead waters allow you to hang a fly over salmon in a very taking way at times. I have experimented in summer fishing on a very long slow pool on the Endrick with a light sinking line and small salmon flies and have accounted for several good salmon and in the evening for numbers of big sea trout. Floating line on this particular pool takes very few salmon (I don't know why) and only takes smallish sea trout of up to three pounds.

There are times in summer and autumn, particularly when sea trout are in dead waters, that handlining of a fairly vigorous sort is a very good way to present your flies to the fish. I have a great pleasure in long hauling – stripping in line with the left hand in long slow draws – to give a steady progress of about a yard every two seconds, then a pause of about a second while the hand reaches out for the line and commences the hauling again. One has to be careful in hooking fish too in a long hauling technique. Too often a raising of the rod and a spasmodic haul of the line either disengages the fish or smashes the tackle.

Dry fly on dead waters for sea trout has usually disappointed me. Fish come up to a dry fly from time to time, but the rise is usually a splashy wallop at the floater rather than a take. Even in calm conditions I would expect a sea trout by day to take a small greased line fly, even a trout nymph far better than a floater. In addition a small greased line fly can make attractive use of a slow dragging presentation downstream while a dry fly fished upstream is hindered by drag when it happens.

Lies in dead waters present a real problem to the angler. Where in all that inscrutable canal-like stretch are salmon or sea trout to lie? If a fish shows, mark it, of course, but don't take such indications that these are the only lies. As an angler used to fishing new waters I have come to look carefully at the configuration of the banks in plotting lies. In dead waters look carefully for narrowing down of the river, especially after a wider section in which fish have been seen splashing. My reason for being so specific about this is that salmon splashing in a deeper pool in the dead waters may not be takers but where the current concentrates at the tail of a dub like that there is sure to be a lie for a fresher fish more likely to take your fly.

Where banks have caved in during floods you can often find a clue to another lie in dead water. The stream immediately above the collapsed bank is likely to be slightly faster than the surrounding water and to give some comfort to a salmon. If this stream is on a curve, as it so often is, fish it from its concave side if possible and using a long line, mend hard and get the fly to fish slowly off the lies into the shallower water on your side.

There is no doubt at all that dead waters pose special problems, but my experience of them suggests that they are good yielders of fish provided the water's few clues can be read to the angler's better briefing. It is comforting to find Thurso anglers who swear by the dead waters and who kill many fish in them. The Thurso club waters have long stretches in this category. This beat yields fish well in summer. The lower four beats of the Thurso have the distinction of having provided by far the best bags of summer and autumn salmon, one beat last August yielding fifty in a day of unprecedented sport.

Dead waters, for me, have that charm of mystery about them, which some streams and pools forfeit by being easier to read and fish. For me they are in no sense 'dead' but merely waters presenting slightly fewer clues to the fish lies and the fishing techniques than other stretches. It may well be the loch fisher in me that warms to these special river problems. Certainly some loch techniques provide a basic method of approach. I think the dead waters of a river, however, have their own techniques demanding a knowledge of both flowing water and still water in making the most of the fishing they can provide.

CHAPTER TWELVE

On Seeing Salmon Water

You might think that the experienced angler standing on the banks of a river he knows well would have the finest possible sight of the lies of fish in the water. No one would deny that he sees a great deal, and further, that he can interpret a great deal more from what he sees on the surface. But two or three times in the last few seasons I have had the chance to wade carefully over pools and streams in periods of abnormally low water and I have been, each time, astonished at the difference between what I confidently thought the lies looked like and what I actually found them to be. What I had *not* seen from the bank was critical.

There is a pool on the Tay with a great gravel island constricting the stream between its stones and the long bank of boulders and shingle on the far shore. The stream forges a hundred yards down through this stony neck and strikes the right bank in a very keep pot with eddies, before coursing down the bank for perhaps a hundred and fifty yards more and spending itself in the flats of the long pool tail. From this right bank, with a strong deep stream at one's feet it is easy to look out over the whole pool and think of it as a wide and deep flowing sea fifty yards wide across providing lies for numbers of fish in ideal holding water.

Last June I was fly fishing this stream from the left bank, and in the very low water conditions I found I was able to wade out from the shingle bank. I had seen several salmon splashing well over towards the deep stream on the far side and I felt that if I could get out far enough I would be able to cover them easily. The water deepened round my thighs and rose higher. I paused. Would it be prudent to wade further?

I took two further steps and found the shingle, which looked uniform, suddenly getting shallower. In five yards I was back to knee level and I was wading out over a long submerged ridge of shingle which filled the bulk of the middle of the pool. There were pots in the shingle here and there, little waves and pockets of stones. I had almost crossed the entire pool before I struck the very deep channel I described earlier right in under the far bank. What I had thought to be a sea of great depth consisted of one channel perhaps eight or ten feet deep rapidly shallowing to a great central plateau of gravel flanked on the shingle shore by a channel five or six feet deep. So all my long casts to cover the holding lies in the middle were in fact fishing water of no great depth at all.

My view from the bank suggested that salmon would lie in the middle because I thought it was deep, holding water. I caught six or eight fish from that supposedly deep holding water on the basis of this reasoning. If I had thought it was so shallow I would perhaps have spent less time fishing there. But from my view from the bank I thought the stream looked like holding water; I caught fish there and I expected more. My insight was right, but my view of the pool configuration was grossly wrong.

Have you ever fished a bridge pool, then scanned the same water from the bridge above? How different the water looks from each angle! Next time you take the Soutra road to Jedburgh and Carter Bar, stop at the new Ancrum bridge and look into the Teviot. The pool between the bridges is well known to me, both as a salmon water and as a trout and grayling reach. From the angler's viewpoint as he wades down under the arch of the old bridge just above the new bridge pool, the water is a gentle stream, deepening to a lie behind the old bridge stanchion. Beyond this the stream is much deeper, and brisker and it is here that one expects the salmon to lie. From the new bridge, the one you will no doubt lean over some day soon to check on my assessment, the real story of the pool is discovered. There is a large central bank of mud and stones with a good growth of weed on it. The stream under the right bank arch of the bridge above you looks thin and empty and the stream under the left arch of the same old bridge looks like good trouting water but little else. Where are the salmon? Immediately above the stanchion of the new bridge the shallow shingly stream forms a little hollow in the gravel. There I have seen several springers lying together; there in summer I have seen grilse. I have had a good springer from that little dip (I discovered it by accident in this way). From an angler's wading view of the pool, the stream seems to be the place to fish; from a gazer's point of view from the bridge, the surprise holding lie in the gravel is revealed.

The surface of a stream is a good, but limited pointer to the shape of the bottom, but from an angler's point of view on the bank, or wading into the river, the surface conceals more than it reveals of the real lies. Experience helps in making proper assessments, but experience cannot legislate for quirks in the bottom not specially signalled by surface markers.

I remember once exploring a rocky stretch of the Doon where I had noticed, on several occasions, salmon showing in what I took to be shallow trout water. I waded out over a flattish shelf of rock and almost stumbled into a narrow, deep fissure with gravel at the bottom. It was four or five feet deep and the approach from both banks was shallow streamy water eighteen inches to two feet deep. I reckon an angler would have had to stumble into this crack to discover it. It was well worth a wetting, I can tell you. I had three salmon out of it in the course of one season.

But let me describe one superb sea trout pool on the Border Esk. It is on a private stretch of the river, but like all the middle Esk in summer, association or private, is teeming with sea trout. This middle pool has a long slow 'dub' with sandy and stony bottom. You fish it from the tail. You wade out from the right bank over sandy and shingly bottom then about ten yards out you turn upstream and you follow a sandy ridge which takes you another ten yards up into the pool. From this point you can cast a long line right under the far bank where there is a deep gentle stream right under the grass. Handlining flies quickly from the very roots of this grass takes the most magnificent sea trout in the dusk and the dark. The taking place is, I'll swear, less than a foot from the left bank and the best of it is only fishable from the point of access I mention. From the other side, the angler on the bank would see the lie. It would be under his feet, would be fishable only on the dangle with the consequent plucking and loss of fish; would be hard to fish in summer anyway, with long grass and other vegetation between you and the water. In short, the location of the fish and the fishing of this narrow highly productive band of water depends on one having actually waded the pool tail and having taken the trouble to study the pools one fishes at night in broad daylight, plotting lies and positions in the light of actual depths, strength of stream and the like.

It is just this surprise element in where fish lie that makes fishing fascinating. The tiny stream on the South Esk at Cortachy where my host insisted there would be a salmon. I cast and the fish rose in what I would have thought was only inches of water. It rose twice; I missed it twice – or it missed me. Later I discovered a little holding basin in the stream bed. Or again, the lie pointed out to me in the weedy pool of beat 15 of the Thurso. In a pool not well marked at all on its surface, salmon have distinct preferences for certain tiny and well defined areas of it. I have since then taken three salmon from one of these lies pointed out to me by Dan Murray, who knows the bed of the stream if anybody knows it.

When you stand on the bank, then, looking at your beat with the eye of a stout Cortez, remember that your viewpoint is famous for what it reveals about the water in the light of your own experience, but it is also a limited view of the water you are to fish. Water conceals from one angle what it reveals to another. What you cannot see is probably critical.

CHAPTER THIRTEEN

On Seeing Salmon

Few salmon anglers like to fish their beats without seeing salmon showing in some way during the day. On some rivers to see salmon splashing in certain ways is a bad sign; on others to see the same sort of movement is a first class indication that taking fish are in the lie. Seeing salmon is an integral part of salmon fishing and it might be useful to try to outline some of the ways salmon show and to say how, in my experience, these showings are related to takes.

On smaller rivers in the west of Scotland, where I served my apprenticeship in salmon fishing, to see fish was a bad thing. The local saying was, 'If you can see a salmon, you won't hook it; it is the salmon which doesn't show that you hook'. I believe this, like many other local sayings, to be a dangerous half truth.

On smaller rivers you often find that the lies are comparatively insecure. Many are shallow and most are fishable by normal angling techniques. Salmon in them are therefore subjected to disturbances which fish in a large river would be free of.

This is one reason why fish which show readily on the small rivers mentioned are often uncatchable. They are showing in a disturbed way. Typical of this disturbed rise is the splashy lunge. The fish shows with half its length out of the water and makes a slosh on the surface. Often the slosh or lunge type of rise is preceded by a vigorous boil on the surface. Fish disturbed by anglers' lures will sometimes act like this.

Similarly, fish disturbed by other salmon will slosh about on the surface. On one magnificently well stocked pool on the Endrick, where one may find several hundred salmon all trying to find a peaceful lie after passing over the falls at the

Netting a good sea trout from the Border Esk. The date July; the angler, the author

Above: The $9\frac{1}{2}$ lb. salmon taken on Loch Assapol, Island of Mull, which is described in Chapter 18. *Below:* Three sea trout from a night's catch to one rod (the author). River: The Sheil. Weights: $8\frac{1}{2}$ lb., 6 lb., $5\frac{1}{4}$ lb. The fish took a No. 8 Dark Mackerel fly (like a Mallard and Claret) fished at night on a floating line

Pots of Gartness, salmon are famous sloshers and boilers. I have fished the pool with the surface never still from disturbed rises. It is interesting to watch the change that overtakes the pool in the evening.

There is often a period of comparative peace as the light fades. Usually you kill a fish about this time. Early morning also brings this kind of taking calm.

On larger rivers like the Tay I am convinced that it is a good thing to see fish move. Several times this season I have been fishing down a pool and have seen out of the corner of my eye a salmon splashing. Admittedly, it has usually been a quick little splash as if the fish had popped its head out of the water with its chin. On at least three occasions this season I have backtracked ten yards or so, cast out my spoon (or in one case fly) and have taken a fish – probably the same salmon.

On both larger and smaller rivers there are ways a salmon will show and predict a take. I like salmon to show like trout. Occasionally the fish will show, make little rings on the surface like good trout, or showing a fin in the middle of the ring. My hopes soar when I see this, for this is perhaps the finest showing sign of all and is almost certainly an indication of a taking fish. I saw a pool on the Thurso with several fish like this one April. The fish were fresh and the evening, although cold, was calmer than it had been all day. I took a fish from the pool tail, then fishing from the small bridge over the stream of the same pool I dabbled a fly, and raised a fish then took one – a spendidly fresh ten-pounder, before the light went and the fish stopped rising.

In August on the Tay I arrived at the water early and found a splendid rise of salmon going on. These rises were more head-and-tail movements rather than the trout rises I mention, but they were trout-like and definite takers. I spun through the pool hoping for a quick fish to the bait and I touched nothing. The rise continued and I realised that I was probably fishing below the salmon. I quickly mounted my greased line fly outfit and at the fourth cast over the area I raised and hooked a splendid little fish of six pounds.

Running salmon are a sight to thrill any angler – or indeed any lover of nature. These splendid fish forging up through rapids and leaping falls display an urgency in their movements which never fails to grip one. I believe the rule of thumb which says that one never catches a running fish. But I am quite certain that as a fish stops for a breather, even for a breather of a minute or a few seconds, it is one of the most takable fish in the pool. I saw a run of fish going through a pool on the beat I was fishing on the Tay once and the slack water beyond the heavy stream, where there was some respite from the powerful force of the current, was boiling with fish at one point. I dashed down for my spinning rod (I had been fly fishing the stream) and put a Toby out to the slack water in which the fish were congregated. The second cast produced a sixteen-pounder with sea lice on. By the time this was killed, and safely ashore in the hut, the run had dwindled and ceased. Perhaps twenty fish in a small batch had moved upstream, and I had been lucky to take one of them. Fish showing like this in a known resting place below a fast neck or below a small fall are often well worth our interest, for a taker can be found among them.

Running fish often delude you, however. If you are at the tail of a pool and you see repeated head and tail rises of what might be different fish you are almost certainly seeing fish running up into the pool. Such fish will not take your lures at all. The running head and tail rise can only be detected by experience. The place of the rise and the sliding motion of the fish betray the runner. Anglers often spend hours on a pool tail fishing over what they think are a few fish heading and tailing in a taking way, only to find that they are covering a showing point for runners entering the pool. The best place to be when you see this kind of rising is on the stream at the head of the pool, where you may be able to spot the resting lies and take a fish as it pauses. Sometimes a runner taken in a resting spot turns out to be a very tired fish indeed. Sometimes it turns out to be a very hard fighting and splendidly strong, fresh fish.

But what are we to say of the showing of 'resident' salmon in a pool? Fish which have occupied lies for some time, and which may, in a river like the Tweed or Tay, be spring fish as black as coal by the middle of summer, often show in a way which makes the angler wonder whether the fish is a taker or not. Many a fruitless hour has been spent covering stale fish which show from time to time throughout the day and excite the fisher. Sometimes the rise is a boil with one or two centres. The single centred boil is usually a tail boil with fish turning over some way below the surface. The double-centred boil is an upheaval nearer the surface which would produce a main boil and a tail boil.

Neither is a very useful sign. The only way you could be sure that the fish was stale, of course, would be to see part of it. I have a fairly quick eye for spotting the tell-tale colour of a stale fish, but even with some experience of seeing these salmon, it is possible to go far wrong. I remember one fish which showed in silhouette and I took it to be stale, since it showed black against the matt grey of the water behind. I caught another sight of the salmon from another angle later and, taking it to be the same fish, saw it to be splendidly clean and silvery.

On a beat one gets to know well there are salmon which you practically doff your hat to, so familiar do they become. I remember one fish among all the kelts of spring which I used to see day after day in one of our main lies. She was a baggot, that is a large unspawned salmon, one which for reasons best known to herself had failed to shed her eggs in winter and was still full in spring. She had good colour, this hen, and to an inexperienced eye may well have looked like a fresh fish up a few weeks.

One of my less experienced friends came clambering down the bank to where I was fishing one day. 'Bill, what's this I've caught – kelt or fresh fish?' He was holding the baggot I had nodded to in the stream above. She was alive and a nice looking fish of about fifteen pounds. We tried to revive her and give her her freedom, but she was too weak. Baggots, of course, are regarded by some anglers as fair game, and they look well and often eat surprisingly well. My friend took this one and reported that his family enjoyed it, that it looked splendid and brought him the kudos of having taken a springer!

On beats where salmon seldom show, I find myself longing for the sight of a fish, even a non-taker. I know factors and keepers like guests to see salmon. Psychologically, it is a good thing. But, as we have seen, in some cases the sight of salmon is a sign of sport ahead. But sport or no sport, salmon moving in

75

their pools have taken me to the waterside on many a Sunday, when, of course, salmon angling in Scotland is forbidden. I have lain and watched in fascination as the fish moved. For me, the moving of salmon has a compulsion and an excitement which few other natural activities have.

CHAPTER FOURTEEN

Fishing Overcrowded Pools

There is a strong case for arguing that every pool has its optimum number of salmon and that carrying a heavier stock of fish than this makes for poor angling conditions. This is particularly true of rivers which are adding weighty summer runs to existing spring ones. The form on many such rivers is that the spring run fills up the upper reaches and the potted fish take up most of the better lies. There they lie more or less uncatchable except in falling water after spates when they have been gingered up, or tempted to run a pool or two further upstream. These residents seem to mix rather badly with fresh incomers and most of us have had the experience of fishing in late summer when there was every indication of fresh fish moving up into our water, yet the air seemed to be filled with red leaping salmon, sloshing and leaping from known lies. This display is usually the result of territorial dispute over lies between established residents and incoming fish and makes fishing very much less productive than it might be.

I have seen clear cases of this kind of overstocking on Tweed and I have watched fresh fish being taken from the most unlikely lies as a result of this lie overcrowding. It seems to me that cases of gross disturbance in a pool ought to send the angler down to other water where fresh fish can rest without facing the disturbances of the usual pool lies. I saw a boy on Tweed, crowded off the holding pool on an association stretch by adult anglers fishing a thin glide a hundred yards below the pool and take a fresh fourteen pounder and lose a second fish.

In a slightly different category I know of a long flat, three to four feet in depth, below a magnificent holding pool. Salmon are taken in the pool (on the River Sheil) but when summer comes there are either resident sea trout large enough to defend themselves against salmon, or resident spring salmon, and summer fish are taken generally on the glide below the pool proper. Dispossessed fish occupy lies that are shallower, but lies that are often better fishing water. I mean by that that the lies in a gravelly glide are eminently suited to long greased line work of a classic sort while lies in the bodies of pools are often difficult to fish because of turbulence, boulders, etc. In addition, shallower lies are far more productive from the fly fisher's point of view.

The signs that a pool is becoming overcrowded are worth watching for. Usually salmon show in an agitated way and this spectacle is for many anglers an inseparable part of late summer and autumn fishing. Salmon disturbed from a lie may show suddenly, and violently in long straight leaps. These may or may not be preceded by a series of vigorous boils on the surface indicating the driving off of one fish by another. Again, the salmon that is disturbed might show head-and-tail, but in a different kind of way to the head-and-tail rise beloved of anglers as the sure sign of a taking fish. The disturbed head-and-tail rise is high in the water with plenty of other fish showing. It can be very fast, like a thwarted leap. In cases of gross disturbance it is persistent and anglers who have shared my experience of hooking a good fish in a lie and losing him without taking him far from his holt will no doubt have seen displays later in the day of the fish showing persistently in a fast head-and-tail rise indicating disturbance. I had a great display of this once on the Doon when a fish in an inaccessible lie below me tugged, like an unruly dog until the hook came out. Half an hour later he began showing up and down like a shop window display. He was of course a disturbed fish, not a taker. Another persistent head-and-tailer – a lost fish of mine again – broke my spinning line in a spate and rose in a pool on the River Ayr until he became a local spectacle. His high head-and-tailing with the trace at times clearly seen attracted at least one poacher with a sniggle.

One might profitably recall the true head-and-tail rise which is a likely prelude to a take. It is low in the water and the back slides slowly through the surface. Often I have seen only a fin break and a ripple like a trout rise break inside the dumb waves of the bulge. This is exciting movement calculated to give many of us who should know better, 'the shakes' of the tyro.

In late summer I accept the dictum given to me as a boy that you should always fish for the salmon that does not show. This is a local rule applying mainly to medium sized spate rivers where lies filled up very quickly and from August onwards the stock of succeeding runs disturbed the residents, sending salmon flying in all directions in spectacular disarray. A more mature rule might be to fish only where salmon were showing 'like good trout' or in known resting lies where fish were not persistently showing in a disturbed way.

It used to be one of the greatest frustrations to me to find my pools full of fish and to come away at night empty handed. The only bonus I got was an occasional fish that slashed at my fly and hooked itself under the chin or worse, in the tail. Occasionally when I had turned to sea trout in the evening a salmon would be the first taker, beginning the evening's sport at the tail of a pool. Now in late summer I fish crowded water in lies well above the main splashing in the pools, and well below them, even trying trout runs and individual potholes known to me as lies for very small numbers of fish. There can be too many fish in the pools of the later season.

One final point might be of value for the late summer fisher. Spring fish already on known redds are liable to make spectacular displays as other spawners arrive. These are of course stale fish and not worth casting for. In addition, one should as far as possible after the end of August leave hens alone to spawn, returning any so ill advised as to take your fly. The activity on redds is not conducive to sport. Certainly a large fly will bring on attacks at times, particularly by makes, and fish will 'take' the fly. More often they will foul hook themselves by attacking the intruder. Redds are clearly defined on many waters and keepers will guide a new rod to a beat. Certainly for best late sport one should cover the running lies in pool tails, or the waiting lies in streams above pools. There, there is at least the chance of a fresh fish. I would take it that this is what we are really fishing for.

CHAPTER FIFTEEN

Salmon Takes and Mis-Takes

It seems to me, looking back over some years of salmon fly fishing, that there are many baffling facets of salmon takes. Not the least of these is the inability I have often found to hook salmon offers after the fish have definitely been moved by the fly and have shown themselves in what appears to be a good take. Other fly-fishers I have spoken to about this confirm that they also have had the same experience, particularly in summer fishing. Fish move to the fly in several ways, but a great number of the offers do not lead to any kind of contact whatever with the fish.

Salmon are sometimes not hooked because of sheer bad fishing, of course, and those of us who have more or less quick physical responses are often far too fast on the strike. This, of course, is a fault as old as the hills. Young salmon fishers are often taught to fish the fly steadily, clamping the line to the rod with the fingers of the right hand and holding in the left hand a hank of line which is to be released as soon as there is a take.

This line releasing does two things. Principally, it stops the keen young salmon fisher striking his fish as if the salmon were a large trout. Secondly, it gives the fish way to go down with the line which can then belly out below the salmon and by the weight of the current pull the hook home. In this way of dealing with salmon takes lies the answer to hasty-handedness.

But it is still true that many of the summer takes we have to the fly never result in proper contact. Let me give an example. In late July I was fishing the Ross-shire Blackwater – the Carron tributary – and after a rise of about 9 in. the water was in splendid fly-fishing fettle. In one long, slow pool below a shallow, fast stretch of river perhaps 20 salmon had collected and were in the lies, heading and tailing in a most tantalising manner. I remember my vivid impression, on seeing this activity, was that I was certain to have half a dozen fish during the day.

I was using a floating line and a sea-trout cast with No. 10 wet flies and I fished these, greased-line style, down the well-rippled surface of the pool. In about half an hour I had moved five of the fish to the small flies, and it was heart-stopping to see the beautiful head-and-tail rises my flies provoked, but no fish made any contact with me. I know it was not bad reaction in this case because with a floating line there was a permanent indication of any merest touch to the flies. I am sure the tail fly was the one causing all the interest – it was a Wickham, No. 10 – and I am also fairly certain that the fish moved past the fly very close to it, but not over it. It was fishing about 3 in. down.

I retired to work out other tactics, and throwing normal advice to the wind about changing down and down until a fish took, I put on a No. 8 Tod fly, a rough Loch Lomond version of a Brown Turkey. Beginning in the stream, I had a splash and a pluck, and then, half-way down the pool, I had a beautiful take which I somehow managed to bungle by taking the fly out of a willing mouth. The fish came again and definitely missed, and I cast again with my heart pounding, determined to give the fish plenty of time.

At that moment I was interrupted by the arrival of two boys on the bank who had been fishing for trout above me. I called to them that the salmon were moving well, and I was reminded that I was in fact covering one by the solid pull of a salmon well hooked. It was the same fish as I had just missed, and this time was hooked well back in the mouth on the Tod fly. It was 8½ lb., almost fresh run.

I link this with a series of experiences a friend of mine had on the Awe about the same time. He found fish moving because of the fly, but not moving sincerely to the fly. He got to the stage of being able to predict when the explosive boil would come to his fly, but this type of rise was never the prelude to a hooking.

Anglers have talked for many years about salmon takes and the theories they have produced are many. I wonder, however, whether there might not be some truth in two of them – truth relevant to the situations we have described. If a salmon moves *at* a fly rather than *to* it there is a strong case for saying that the fish is disturbed or irritated by the fly. Some would have us believe that this is the motive for salmon reaction at all times. I believe many of the head-and-tail rises I have had have been disturbed rises.

Salmon head-and-tail when they first come into a pool and when they have not yet settled fully into the lies. Salmon also head-and-tail when they are disturbed by wading. So often a salmon will be seen heading and tailing when another fish is being played. Again, I have seen heading and tailing when a large bait has been dropped into a low summer lie. All this would appear to have a pattern in it, associating the head-and-tail rise with disturbance or fear, and this would perhaps be behind the ancient piece of wisdom that counsels us to change down for such a fish until there is a sincere take.

But the other taking theory which throws light on the behaviour of these summer fish is the idea that salmon only take when a reflex feeding action is triggered off. Thus it might be held that the first reaction of a disturbed salmon would be to drown the intruding fly or at least attack it, but the second reaction would be to eat it. In many summer cases the salmon that eventually takes the fly into his mouth does so very gingerly indeed. It is not unusual for an angler to hook three or four fish lightly and lose them all in half a minute or even less.

This could readily be explained as a tentative attempt to eat the creature which had disturbed the salmon or a smaller version of that creature. This kind of take, lightly hooking the fish, is often associated with previous boiling of fish at the fly.

One cannot rule out the effect of fast water on the fly causing these badly hooked effects. Summer fish often lie in the necks of streams, and it is not easy to present a fly slowly and carefully to such lies. The salmon may rise, but the stream whips the fly across its mouth and at best grips the fish by a skin hold far forward in the mouth. Many anglers swear by small tube flies with No. 12 or even No. 14 trebles which have a splendid grip on fish even far forward in the mouth.

Thinking of my own past fish in Scottish waters, I am convinced that the bulk of the sincere takes have been deep. Even to floating line the takes have often been through salmon sucking the fly in and turning away without the spectacular head-and-tail rise to the fly. It seems to be the difference between sincerity and ostentation. The slow taking fish does its job quietly and efficiently and hooks itself if it is given time to turn away and draw the hook home. The fish which shows to the fly may take, but may not touch the fly at all because it is a disturbed fish. If the disturbed fish does take the fly he is often lightly hooked.

CHAPTER SIXTEEN

Give Him Line and Scope

On one beat of the Tay which I have fished regularly through the season two anglers have in recent seasons had the alarming experience of having their line entirely taken out. In one case the fish was landed; in the other, things did not turn out so well. Both battles emphasise the immense power of a big salmon in a river like the Tay where there is room for the fish to manoeuvre.

The first fish was a springer, hooked in a well known lie in the main stream of a large pool. During the earlier fight the fish showed itself to be strong, but did not behave aggressively. It looked like offering a hard fight, but not a dashing one. As so often happens, however, the salmon 'woke up' after the first quarter of an hour and began to take long runs downstream, and the angler had no option but to follow the fish as well as he could down banks not noted for their easy pathways. That salmon continued downstream for eight hundred yards and took the best part of an hour to kill. It was a very fresh springer of 33½ lb., the kind of fish the Tay is world-famous for – a salmon second to none anywhere.

The second fish was an autumn one, one of the clean very large cock salmon which the Tay from Dunkeld to the sea produces from September onwards. This fish was hooked at the tail of the pool above the fastest neck of water on the whole beat. This fast neck of water fished from the right bank is a difficult piece of wading at the best of times, but when one is plunging downstream in pursuit of a really heavy fish, it is something like a watery trap.

This autumn fish, like many of its weight, hardly seemed to mind being hooked for the first two runs or so. It sidled powerfully away from the angler and crossed the wide pool, taking sixty yards of line in a steady, unstoppable, but not spectacular way. Pumping moved the fish back and the whole thing was repeated. After the second hard pumping operation the salmon. showed on a short line almost in the lie it had been hooked in, close to the angler's bank. It was, on the estimate of two experienced fishers, a fish between forty and forty-five pounds, as clean as a springer and impressively thick. Seeing a fish like this is almost always a bad thing. It produces what one friend of mine calls 'the shakes'.

The problem here was whether to anticipate the fish and move downstream first, playing the fish on a longer line initially, but at least being in a position to follow hard should the fish turn and run down the long fast neck with its very difficult wading. My friend on this occasion decided to test his own luck and hope for the fish staying in the pool above. All went well for about twenty minutes and a gentle optimism began to pervade the operation. Then as if it had only been toying with the business so far, the fish turned and ran down the fast water below. There is a stretch of some two hundred and fifty yards of really brisk, deep water between the gravel island and the left bank and below this is a fine open pool with shingle. If one could only reach that, all might be well.

In a crisis like this, the first thing most of us would do would be to run downstream and make as much ground as possible, following the salmon and, if possible, recovering line. This fish tore off at a tremendous rate and the drum of the fixed spool reel was soon almost bare. At this point the angler, winded by stumbling down through the edge of the deep fast water, decided to try that old trick of throwing off his spool pick-up and letting the line run free. This often makes the salmon slow down or stop and, with line gathering below him in the current, may create pressure on the fish downstream and make the fish move back up again. It's a good tactic. I've seen it work well. This time, it merely hastened the complete stripping of the spool. Two hundred yards of eighteen pound nylon were all but gone.

My friend, by this time, had resigned himself to a final tug o' war and a break, and bracing himself, he watched the last of the line run off, and waited for the twang. Nothing happened.

The line tightened and tightened, stretching for what seemed a ridiculous time. Then it sagged slack, with little drama. The trace had broken at the swivel knot, two hundred yards away below him, obviously the weakest part of the whole tackle.

These two remarkable fish are exceptional, but there may be a lesson or two in them for the fighting of any salmon. I'm a great believer in not allowing a salmon to take charge of you in a fight, and with the general run of fish in the teens of pounds there is little reason for letting a fish take all the line he can, particularly if he is off downstream. A salmon hooked well in the mouth will not usually take more than forty or fifty yards in a single rush, and if he makes one of these in his first few minutes he is likely to come in jolly quickly immediately afterwards. I saw a springer of fifteen pounds take nearly ninety yards of line in one superb rush, but the fish had little more to offer. Its later fight was largely dogged circling as the line was recovered by pumping.

Most of us will recognise the phenomenon of the salmon that 'wakens up' after behaving in a fairly docile manner. I had two fish in quick succession one day which behaved in this extraordinary way. They took and gave a good pull (I was spinning) and thereafter were prepared to be brought in right to my feet without so much as a splash on the surface. Dull creatures they were for the first few minutes. Both fish changed radically when they found themselves in the shallower water near my feet. It may be that the fish saw me too. I can't say, but both raced off in a second stage of the fight which tried the quality of the hook hold to the maximum and gave me several anxious moments before the salmon eventually came in to the tailer. In one of these cases the very fast part of the fight ended suddenly when the fish turned over exhausted after a spectacular few moments of surface lashing.

The time honoured advice on playing fish, as Shakespeare's metaphor puts it, is to give him line and scope. I disagree with this to some extent. Give him scope, yes. Let him have water and time to lunge, dive, pull and show, but only let your fish take what you judge to be a reasonable amount of line. Only a novice lets a salmon draw off line *ad lib.* and move far downstream. This leads to disaster. Firstly, it can be very difficult to recover line, even by following down a fairly clear bank.

Secondly, the angle on the hook hold becomes dangerous the further a fish drops down below you. I once watched a huge fish I had hooked on the Spey backing slowly down a pool and reaching the fast water below. I lost him, for the second reason I give above. In that case I could not follow readily, and like the Tay fish I described earlier, he was a massive fish, able to dictate to me. But I have seen mere nine pounders straighten out hooks once they had got well down stream of a rod and had used the water pressure to add power to their own pulling.

A fish of over 30 lb. was landed from the same lie on the Spey as I hooked my big fish in. The second fish did exactly what I described, backing down the fast stream and obliging the angler to follow. Luckily the rod was on the other bank of the river and pursuit was possible. It took over an hour to get the fish to the gaff – two pools below. Backing down is very often the sign of a really heavy fish (or a foul hooked one!).

Many of the 'monster' salmon hooked and lost on our rivers (particularly in autumn) are foul-hooked fish. Foul hooking is most likely in the late autumn when fish are thick in the pools, and when our flies and spinners are fished rather more deeply than in the summer. A fish foul-hooked in the tail often fights with a fantastic speed and power, and it may go absolutely berserk, running out of the water on the far shore, for instance. It may leap wildly, and it may take a great deal of line. But a tail-hooked fish will 'drown' if you tire him and get his head downstream.

The fish hooked in the back is the worry. It is in charge of you if it is a salmon of any size at all. If it decides to lie doggo, you will be snagged into the fish and may (as I saw on Tweed once) have to break the line. If the fish decides to move downstream, nothing you can do will stop it. Many of the tales of enormous fish hooked, run and lost are of foul-hooked ones, and they are most certainly better lost as famous fish, than landed as mediocre, foul-hooked salmon. On many beats all such fish are returned to the water and most clubs have strict regulations to this end. But one can, occasionally, foul-hook a fish inadvertently, get a marvellous fight out of it, and feel that the sport was of greater merit than the fight with the mouth-hooked fish.

I had such a fish once on Loch Maree. I raised a salmon

twice and missed, then had a lovely head-and-tail take. The fish fought brilliantly, taking line well out into the loch. I have an undying memory of white backing stretching alarmingly far out into the black waters, and of my rod bowed hard under the strain. The fish was a fresh 15 pounder, hooked in the root of the tail. I killed it, for I had raised it, hooked it, as I thought, well, and had played it in a fight of great sporting value – a fight in which the odds were definitely on the side of the fish far more than if the salmon had been mouth-hooked.

Perhaps there is no simple rule at all to cover an activity as unpredictable and varied as playing salmon. Nevertheless no harm would be done by the average angler if he reversed Shakespeare's advice. By all means give your fish scope in the fight, but only give him what line he insists on taking. Give him that line readily, but don't give an inch more than the fish insists on. Too much line in the water is a hazard successful salmon fishing cannot afford.

Above: Fly fishing the good stream at Peel Bridge, near Ashiestiel, River Tweed. This is a good autumn water, but summer and spring fish are also taken. Ashiestiel was for many years the home of Sir Walter Scott. Angler: Mr W. H. Conn. *Below:* Captain Moller plays a 12-pounder hooked in the Junction Pool of Tweed at Kelso. Time, February

Looking wistfully at a scene from recent history. A local angler looks at the Cruives Pool Inverawe, on the River Awe, Argyllshire. The water was running at 32 inches on the gauge. Under the regulated water conditions produced by the hydro electric scheme this pool may never again carry this height of water, 13–15 inches being more likely

Mr Rob Wilson of Brora fishes the Ford Pool of the Lower Brora. This is one of the most delightful and most productive rivers of the Highlands, with some tremendous fly fishing water

CHAPTER SEVENTEEN

Fly v. Spinning: An Explanation

I ought to confess right away that I have a grave weakness of character as an angler. I have an unstoppable inclination to draw at least tentative conclusions from the incidents of my fishing year. Recently I have been turning in my mind the question of the ancient war between those who spin a salmon water on a given day and those who fish it. Most anglers will be aware that fly fishers usually hold that fly fishing is not really much good immediately after spinning.

I think a lot of psychology is involved in this situation. The chap in front of you, you think, really has the cream of the fishing, covering the salmon first and leaving you the ones he has disturbed. When one is alone on a salmon pool, of course, one can be both spinner and fly fisher as it best suits one. This was my lot on my beat of the Tay recently. I arrived early in the morning, found the pool in perfect ply with eighteen inches of fresh water running, on a summer morning with still clear air and a warm temperature. Perfect.

I saw fish splashing in several lies down the long stream that steadily loses pace throughout the pool. One lie attracted me particularly – the little bay above the hut. About half a dozen fish were showing there in a steady and decidedly hopeful way. Greed, or some other base instinct, made me decide to try for a quick first fish by spinning the lie. I set up my L.R.H. 2 and Ambassadeur 6000, attached a $2\frac{1}{2}$ in. brown and gold wooden devon twisted on a spiral lead and started casting.

For an hour I presented the devon to the fish, still rising eagerly, and in the same place. The light flooded in to my benighted mind. Fool! Conditions were perfect for fly fishing and here I was spinning! Further, the salmon were clearly against the devon. I hurriedly set up my spliced rod, used my floating line and cast a No. 2 Hairy Mary out over the lie. Four casts later I had the most perfect head and tail rise you could ever describe and I was into my first fish of the day. Time, seven twenty a.m.

I had fly fished for another three quarters of an hour, raising one more salmon – not such a good taker this time – when I saw that most thrilling sight – a batch of big fish coming splashing up through the pool and stopping in the slack water on the far side of the very fast stream which rushes into the pool at the neck. I could never hope to reach them with my fly rod, and wading was quite out of the question. I reached for my spinning outfit, attached a big copper toby without a weight (although the top stream is so fast that we often take salmon from it with a weighted trace above a toby) and cast it as far as I could across the water to the resting lie beyond. Second cast and I was into a fish, a splendid fresh salmon of sixteen and a half pounds with sea lice on it. What a fighter! It rose to my toby almost on the surface and took it just like a fly.

Now, take these two fish together and consider their takes. One refused a deeply spun devon, but took a subsequently fished surface (or near surface) fly. The other rose to take a toby high in the water in the same conditions of temperature and water height. Spinning below I suggest in both cases would not have either interested the fish, or disturbed them.

I have seen near-surface flies and lure consistently taking fish when deeper fishing would not turn ten per cent of the salmon moving to the higher lure. I have seen four fish in quick succession take small devons harled right on the surface behind a Tay boat while the bank rods, with weighted devons, tobys, etc., needing the weight for casting, failed to take any. In that case two of the fish referred to rose to near-surface presentation of small devon and a No. 6 Shrimp, harled in water where another rod had just fished for an hour with a really deep bait, actually foul hooking a fish at one point, so deep was his presentation.

Once again, were the taking salmon affected by the deep fishing? Apparently not for the higher fishing following, including the greased line fly, took fish after fish from the same water.

Well, what substance is there in the argument that spinning adversely affects salmon fly fishing? I think it is this. We have described cases of salmon interested in lures at a given *level* taking either flies or spinners *at that level*, and spinning below that level did not affect their willingness to take the appropriate lure when it was presented. I dare say fly fishing at a deeper level would have had the same negative effect, even if the same size fly as the one that took the fish had been used.

Think of the other conditions so often seen, however. Salmon are in the pool, and from time to time are splashing, showing anglers the comparative numbers in each lie. Nothing is taking. (Typical conditions, aren't they!). One angler spins hard over the lie and finding no response, puts on a bigger and heavier minnow or spoon. The fish are persistently harried by a bait swinging over their heads, closer and closer. Watch the movement of fish in such circumstances. The fish rise more often and more vigorously. They may become spectacularly active, but they do not take. Persistent spinning above non-taking fish certainly upsets them, and if we are to believe the theory that holds that at some time during the day salmon will come on to take properly, may we not assume that when the fish are harried by devons presented above them, that they become so agitated that they do not come on to the take.

In a simple rule, salmon that are ready to rise to the top level of the water, will take either fly or bait at that level and will ignore all deeper offerings, and will continue taking for as long as appropriate conditions last, at that level. Salmon not rising at all may be so disturbed by spinning over their heads that they fail to take properly when the time comes.

This is a hypothesis, fitting the conditions I have described on Tay in late summer and early autumn. I have no brief to say it is a universal rule. But it may be. My weakness in wanting to fit theories to what I observe would make me suggest that this interpretation of salmon behaviour might be just as true in Devon as in Perth.

CHAPTER EIGHTEEN

An Island Salmon Loch

In some parts of the northwest highlands, and in many places in the Hebrides, there are trout lochs into which sea trout and salmon struggle by running up burns which you would hardly think capable of covering a finnock. Quite reasonably, you would not expect these to be regarded as important pieces of salmon fishing, and it is no real surprise to find that there are no records of salmon takes, there is no knowledge of where salmon lie and what they might be interested in rising to. But there is another class of Highland and Hebridean loch, where the burn *could* be big enough to carry fish, where respectable numbers of salmon do reach the loch from time to time, yet there is still very little knowledge locally about the movements of salmon, and particularly of the lies they might be found in. One such loch is Assapol, near Bunessan, on the Island of Mull.

I returned to Mull one recent summer for the first time for ten years. I had fished Assapol before, but I found it a somewhat unproductive finnock loch in August, and a disappointing brown trout loch, with few fish over the fingerling size. Few sea trout showed in the loch, and when I asked then about where to drift for them there was really no great detail of drifts or catches available. This time, I decided to spend an afternoon on the water, moving round and more or less surveying the depths and possible drifts, mainly from the point of view of finnock and sea trout, but I had heard of a grilse coming off the loch earlier this summer and I thought that it might be just possible to pinpoint at least one salmon lie in the course of the day.

Surveying is a tedious business, and a waste of fishing time, unless something positive happens. I tried the dap to make finnock show, but this failed to bring up a single fish. I switched to No. 8 sea trout flies, and I mounted a great fuzzy Soldier Palmer on the bob, expecting to work this, bobbing, through the wave and bring up sea trout. Little happened. Twice I had a swirl to the bob and twice I hooked brown trout on it. I began to despair of sea trout being in the loch at all, so I moved ground radically, taking the sheltered bay at the head of the loch rather than the bays and marginal drifts which looked so well rippled further down the loch.

At the top, with the gentler ripple, I changed my cast to a lighter one, tying on a No. 10 Dunkeld on the tail and a No. 8 Dark Mackerel on the bob. Right away I had a sea trout offer and miss, then shortly afterwards I found a finnock of about fourteen ounces and I raised several others. But all this time I had seen no salmon, although I was drifting over water where any salmon movement would have been easy to see. I tried a cast or two off two rocky points and I searched a rocky shore drift that seemed to be good water, but not a fin did I move. Perhaps Assapol salmon were just not there. That burn, I reflected, gummed up with debris and badly needing to be cleaned out, must have prevented even the grilse from getting up. The whole problem of access worried me, and I felt sure that Assapol was just another Hebridean water which no one took any care of, and no one wanted to manage properly, despite the fact that the sea off the burn has excellent harvests of salmon to yield to bag netsmen.

I was, I should mention, alone in the boat with my seven year old and my five year old sons, both of whom were busying themselves with a trout fly rod, taking turns at catching the ever willing fingerlings Assapol brings to trout flies. One boy was beginning to feel cold and to look longingly towards the shore, asking when we would finish. I agreed to make one last drift down the shore to the small boat pier and to call it a none too successful day. Quite suddenly, near a dry stone dyke not far above the pier I saw a salmon move – just a quick little splash seen out of the corner of my eye. Four strokes of the oars took us back over the drift and, using my rod with the lighter cast, since it seemed too much trouble to make a radical change of tackle, I covered the water. First cast, and he came. I had a momentary sight of what looked like a black head positively engulfing my dropper. I tightened and he was hooked.

Thank heaven the wind began to take me off shore, for this turned out to be one of the liveliest salmon I have ever taken on a loch. It stripped line at a great rate of knots and twice made a complete running circle of the boat. Once, after we had drifted forty yards or so away from the lie I had the hair raising experience of the fish turning and deciding that it was going, hell for leather, back to its lie. My fly line rapidly screamed out through the rings, followed by the splice. I remember the feeling of doubt then, a feeling I always get when a splice rattles out, that I may have failed to make a secure whipping of line to backing. Anxieties like this are normal in fishing, and of course, all my double checking of the splice had shown it to be secure . . . but my forehead still wrinkled a bit as I watched the backing go out for more than twenty yards.

The fish stopped in its lie, then yielding to the gentle pressure of the rod from the drifting boat. It followed, and line came back on to the reel fairly easily, thank Heaven! Thereafter the fish began to sound, pulling doggedly, making my *Maxfly* bow in a tight arch. Then the end game began. The salmon came up and began making short runs on the surface and at one point made a half lunge. But the tail was coming up and I knew that, all things being equal, I would likely land the fish.

My two small sons were reacting differently to the fight – the first salmon they had seen me catch. Nicholas, the elder, looked on, seemingly unmoved, only saying from time to time, 'What a long time it takes. I hope you don't lose it after all this!' Mark, the younger boy was bounding up and down with excitement and had twice to be restrained.

I had out with me a Sharpe's spring-loaded gaff, a remarkable piece of tackle, and incidentally, the only gaff I use now. I keep it for boat emergencies like this where a large net is not available and where the tailer is difficult to operate. The Sharpe's gaff is an ingenious piece of tackle. The hook is telescoped down into the shaft and a flexible wire sheath shields the point. There is a trigger on the shaft just below the handle and, at the flick of a thumb, the gaff erects itself with the flexible sheath pushed straight on to shank off the hook.

It is a marvellous gaff for a man like me in a boat, where you only have one hand free, and any fiddling with difficult assembling of a gaff or unfolding a net would spell disaster. The salmon slid towards us and bumped its head, it seemed, on the gunwale of the boat. The gaff went in and the fish was lifted aboard, well over nine pounds in weight, and as far as Assapol went, a kind of nine days' wonder, for very few salmon are taken off the loch each year.

One of the local reactions of my taking this fish was that it seemed remarkable that a fish this size could have got up the burn. The burn is big enough, but the course is choked with old sticks and weeds. No one would, apparently, think of cleaning it out. The fishing tenants are often quite uninterested in the salmon of the loch, some taking the fishing purely because of the shootings. Few people knew anything about drifts or best seasons or flies. I hear that another salmon taken this particular season was wormed out in mid loch, rather in the manner one would bait fish for haddock in Bunessan Bay!

Some Hebridean salmon lochs could be quite good fishings, but they would require management, and that, apparently, would be too much trouble for the owners or tenants. Sea trout and salmon (if any) are regarded as a kind of wild bounty, a gift harvest. How improvident! Sea trout and salmon have to be planted, cared for and harvested like any other crop. If you let rushes and weeds compete with a growing crop, you will make nothing of the harvest. Alas, many fields in Mull show the rushes and weeds virtually taking over from the crops, just as some salmon fishings are, for want of interest largely, left to hang as they grow and produce small returns where really good sport would be possible.

CHAPTER NINETEEN

A Sea Trout Manifesto

Compressing the experience I have had of night sea trout fishing into a few essential practical points is not easy, but anglers new to the sport might find these techniques, discovered over some twenty years of fishing, to be a useful guide to what I consider to be the most exciting form game fishing can take.

1. WHEN TO BEGIN IN THE EVENING

For a safe rule, never begin fishing until it is too dark to tie on a fly without holding it up as a silhouette against the sky. My diaries tell me that we have waited until eleven o'clock in the lightest part of the summer (June in the Highlands) before approaching the pools. In July 10.30 p.m. is a good guide but remember that overhead conditions, and the shade of bank trees make individual differences. If you fish before the night is dark enough you may scare the fish off the feed in the best part of the water.

2. WHERE THE BEST FISHING IS FOUND

For years I operated on the belief that the tails of pools were far and away the best places to fish for sea trout and probably this is the best general rule for those new to night fishing. Sea trout which lie in the safety of deep streams or the wells of pools during the day will come down into the tails of pools in the evening and make furrows on the surface as they move in water often only a foot deep. They will, if they are not disturbed, begin rising to natural fly life in the tails of pools and there a well placed fly will take them in the dark.

Second favourite is the apron of gentle water beyond a stream, especially where trees shield the far bank. Casting over the

Dry fly fishing for trout on the Kalemouth pool of the Teviot

Netting a good Loch Maree brown trout. The brown trout of Maree, like some other large Highland lochs, are scarce, but are excellent when they can be tempted. Month, May. Kinlochewe Hotel boat

Mr R. O. M. Williams sets up his tackle beside the Red Loch in Western Inverness-shire. An hour's hard hill walking was rewarded by a good bag of fish, some of which were well over a pound

stream and pulling the flies steadily away from the feeding fish on the far side often gives wild sport as sea trout slash at flies. The secret here is long casting, a floating line and the ability to control the speed of the fishing flies. This is where precise casting in very poor light conditions is of paramount importance. Too far and you are snagged in the trees, too short and you are not interesting the fish moving in the water beneath the trees.

In the early morning after a night of pool-tailing, sea trout often move back, still feeding, into the faster streams and there I have added several brace to a night's basket after the tails themselves and the aprons beside the streams have become dead.

3. FLOATING OR SUNK FLY?

Some anglers fish a floating fly in the first hour of the evening and a sunk fly thereafter. I have never found the dry fly any better, however, than a 'scuttered' wet fly in the evening. To fish this attractive way, take a well hackled fly, or a 'Parachute' dressing, and fish it on the bob (the top dropper) of your cast. With a floating line, this fly will be the last to sink and at best it will furrow the surface as you fish the flies in. I am a firm believer in fishing the cast slowly for the first yard or so, letting the flies down a little and then stripping faster (about a yard every two seconds) in long pulls causing the dropper fly to surface and cut the water with a furrow. Watch out for a really fierce take to a scuttering fly and remember that the sea trout may be moving fast away from you when you strike. Too many anglers have left perfectly good flies in the jaws of keen sea trout that way. A tightening is all you need.

In slow pools where big sea trout are known to lie – fish of four pounds to double figures of pounds – you may find that the best fish will not come to a fly on the surface. Several times I have found a very deeply sunk fly, fished on a sinking line like a Wet Cel provides the answer. It is fairly tricky fishing and demands certain care in handling fish before the line comes clear of the water after a take. You can lose your fish if you pull too hard against a drowned line with a leaping fish on, and worse, you can permanently damage a rod under the very great pressure you exert against a well sunk line.

4. WHAT FLY SIZE?

This is harder to generalise about than any point. I know waters where July and August fishing gives great sport to a No. 8 sunk fly with a reduction to a No. 10 (large trout) size as the water temperature rises and the level shrinks. I generally operate in two sizes. I fit a tail fly of No. 8 and a dropper of No. 12 (for scuttering) and if fish swirl at the tail fly without taking it I willingly change down to a No. 10. In the middle of the night when darkness is thickest, if fish are still moving, but refusing my smaller flies I change to a special dressing of fly in which a No. 8 sea trout pattern is dressed on a No. 6 low water light salmon iron. This I find often raises fish and hooks them well when smaller flies either fail altogether or bring short rises.

I have several experienced friends who swear by a demon type of lure in the dark reaches of the night. This may be anything from a tandem-mounted trout fly on two No. 10 hooks to a three hook demon with a trailing hackle up to two inches long. Big fish will take demons when other lures fail, but equally, demons can fail to interest rising sea trout which will move to the smaller flies I have mentioned earlier.

5. PATTERNS OF FLY FOR NIGHT FISHING

Far ahead for my sea trout fishing, all Scottish fishing by the way, is the Dunkeld No. 10 or No. 8. The gold body and orange hackle complement well the grouse wing. Most of my best night fish have all taken this fly, perhaps because I have seen such sport with the pattern that I would hardly fish without it. In recent seasons, a Dark Mackerel has rivalled it however. The Dark Mackerel is a variant of the Mallard and Claret, but with a palmer hackle and a fluorescent silk body.*

For river fishing in the north west of Scotland a first class pattern is the *Black Pennell*. This hairy black fly with palmer-style hackles down its body makes a first class dropper fly. *Soldier Palmer*, tied with ginger hackles, can do magnificent execution in Highland streams also. A special pattern tied for one of the finest sea trout fishers I know and combining the values of both Black Pennell and Soldier Palmer is the *Kate*

* Since writing this, Dark Mackerel has topped the poll. Fish it on the dropper with a Dunkell on the tail.

McLaren, basically a *Black Pennell* with a brown hackle at the head. Interestingly enough, two different anglers confided in me recently that they had evolved a magnificent 'secret' pattern of sea trout fly and in each case it turned out to be almost identical with the *Kate McLaren*. This is an indication of a really successful sea trout fly.

On a short list of other flies on which fish have taken well, I suggest *Wickham's Fancy*, again with Palmer-style hackle and a gold body, *Teal and Red*, and *Grouse and Claret*, and in silver bodied flies (which I personally find less successful than gold bodied flies) *March Brown and Silver*.

6. A SPECIAL SEA TROUT ROD?

If you have a trout rod of nine feet in length there is no reason why you should not treat sea trout as unusually heavy trout and fish them with trout rod, reel and line. In fact you may get the best sport this way since far too many people fish enormously stiff, long rods for sea trout thinking of them as small salmon rather than big trout. I have taken most of my sea trout on trout rods, but since I specialise somewhat in summer I have three outfits which give me great pleasure to fish. They are rods and lines I can easily kill grilse and salmon on if I hook them – and one does several times a season while sea trout fishing.

(a) ROD: Sawyer 'Stillwater' parabolic 9 ft. 6 in. canc rod.
LINE: HCH Air Cel, or similar floating line or HCH Wet Cel or similar sinking line. This sinking line is as heavy as I would use on a single-handed trout rod any time. (AFTM8).
CAST: 5 lb. to 9 lb. Kroic nylon according to weight of water, size of fish and size of fly fished – the larger the fly the heavier the nylon of course.

(b) ROD: Sealey 'Maxfly' 10 ft. 3-piece cane rod. This rod has a double-built butt.
(LINES and CASTS as above).

(c) ROD: T. C. Ivens' 'Lake' 10 ft. 2-piece. A butt-actioned rod of great power.
(LINES and CASTS as above).

The lightest rod I have killed sea trout on was an 8 ft. 6 in. hollow fibre glass rod (Milbro F 82s) but I was relieved to get a three pounder ashore on one occasion with this, although it is perfectly suitable for smallish fish. I have also had great sport with an eleven foot rod (Dickson's 'Scott' 11 ft. cane) but I prefer to regard this as a grilse rod rather than a general sea trout rod, excellent though it is for general Highland summer fishing.

Clearly in this 'manifesto' I am trying to bring together my own diverse experience of sea trout and obviously much has been condensed and much has had to be left out. What I would like to impress on new sea trout fishers is that there is no technique in sea trout fishing so authoritative that it cannot be scrapped on a given water or even on a given night. If sea trout are gorging themselves on moths for instance, imitate the food. If you are fishing the estuary of a river or the lower pools where brackish conditions may prevail, fish demons and eel-like streamers since the sea trout may well still be chasing natural bait like this. Finally, learn from your fish and never allow yourself to be dogmatic about a quarry that varies from the shyness of a brown trout at some times to the brashness of a hungry salmon parr at others.

CHAPTER TWENTY

A Floating Line for Night Sea Trout

The floating line at night for sea trout turns the sport from one of tugs in the dark into one of aural and often visual pleasure. Instead of casting out a silk fly line over the tail of the pool where sea trout have been seen rising and splashing, and letting the fly or flies swing round a foot or so under the surface, a floating line makes it possible for the flies to be placed much more precisely, to be held accurately over likely water and to be lifted off the water for the next cast with little or no disturbance.

When a fish is seen rising in the glide at the tail of a pool it is better if the flies can be cast over it at ninety degrees to the flow of the stream, rather than at the so often quoted angle of forty five degrees downstream. As in salmon greased lining, the fly which drifts down over the fish is often much more palatable than the one swung fairly fast over the lie from upstream. The sea trout will rise to the drifted fly readily and will show clearly at the surface when they do. The strike can then be made on seeing or, in the deeper dusk, on hearing the rise. It is better to strike to a mistaken rise than not to strike at all.

It is surprising what one can see at night on the river. The random rising of fish often marks itself by a line of silver against the dark background of the bank opposite. So often it is in such places, against the deep shadow of trees or the overhang of the bank opposite that we find ourselves fishing. Then the wave set up by the rise catches the last of the low light of the dusk and the effect I have described of a line of silver appearing is brought about. One can, of course, see the splashes of vigorous rising fish, and one can hear many of these fish even before we see them. As a general rule one should tighten on every sign of a rise, especially when the activity seems to be from where our flies are.

I fish a light green floater much of the time and I find the visibility of this line splendid. I can tell by its behaviour whether the flies are fishing where they ought or not, and I can tell by the presence or absence of a belly on the line whether the flies are dragging, and whether the line needs mending, that is, rolling a loop upstream to counteract the drag on the line. Some American floating lines are produced in 'moon-glo' and other semi-luminous dressings to make it easier to see the floating line on the pool. I am sure the fish do not mind the colour of the line at all. Indeed, I would very much like to try out a recent line dressing which uses a pigment of very high ultra violet reflecting characteristics. It might make night fishing even more exciting.

The floating line however has advantages when it comes to the hooking of sea trout. Since we tighten when we see the rise we can often calculate from the way the fish has moved, and how fast it took, how quickly or otherwise we must tighten to hook fish well. On a recent night on the Border Esk, out of eight fish, I lost only one, which did not seem to take a very firm hold from the beginning. My companion raised as many fish as I did, fishing a conventional sunk line, but because he had not the control over his strikes owing to the sunk line, he missed half his offers.

In addition, it is delightfully easy to put on the pressure necessary to hook a sea trout well when the line can be lifted cleanly and without dragging from the surface of the pool. The sunk line, before it can be lifted off might well pull the hook out of the initial hold it gained when the fish took.

Some sea trout take immensely quietly at night and there is only a kind of sixth sense feeling in one's fingers that the fish has risen to our flies. I would describe this as a feeling that the line in the hand is somehow heavier, fractionally. With a floating line this feeling is easier to detect than with a sunk line. Time and again I have seemingly plucked a sea trout out of a dead pool purely by the extra sensitivity of the floating line.

A good example of this came recently when, in the doldrums of the night between the dusk and dawn rises when our fish had gone off somewhat, I cast down a stream. I had a strange line feeling that something was moving to me and I struck and hooked a two pounder in the tail. The fun that caused was memorable. What I had felt was a fish rising to the fly, and refusing it, and presumably, sliding its full length along the cast in the take. I do not advocate foul hooking fish, of course, I merely point out that in the pitch dark in a fairly fast stream, even a scrape along the cast can be felt through a floating line.

CHAPTER TWENTY-ONE

Sea Trout: The Taking Prelude

Most sea trout fishers understand by the term 'short taking' that fish either rise to the fly and miss it altogether, or, more infuriatingly, rise to the fly and pluck it, often quite hard, but without making solid contact with the hook point. Theories advanced to account for this include the reflection theory which holds that the fish rise to the image of the fly reflected on the glassy undersurface of the water rather than the fly itself. Others have held that the fish take the tail of the fly only! My own approach to the problem some years ago was to dress sea trout patterns on longshanked salmon hooks and have protruding hooks. It worked, but still had days when there were even shorter takes and fish missed or plucked the fly.

I had a remarkable night in mid-August recently when I had a sort of grandstand seat on the carnival of sea trout takes. It was dusk and dark fishing on the Endrick, beginning at about half past nine in a dull drizzly evening with a pool at good fishing height and well stocked with fish which had arrived during the two previous days from Loch Lomond. They were fresh fish in a relative sense only. I mean by that, none had sea lice, but many were bright silver, having come through the loch in perhaps a week or less. Some of the fish may have been in the loch for up to a month, however.

I fish sunk line on the best of the Endrick I mention. It is part of a carefully studied technique worked out over nearly ten seasons on the water. It took me three years to realise that sea trout there demanded a sunk line and a small fly fished right on the bottom. I still take friends there to fish who say 'Oh yes,' and, mentally noting that I have miscalculated, fish floater. They catch the odd sea trout of the smaller class, say up to two and a half pounds. Those of us who know the pool virtually leger the fly on its sand and gravel bottom and take fish which one year recently ran to a thirteen pounder, and every year run to fish of over nine.

I had the first proper pluck on the occasion I am describing at about nine-thirty. In ten minutes, I had the second. Slipping, I thought; should have hooked one of these. A third strong pluck followed and I found myself looking very critically at the hook points of my Dunkeld No. 8 and my Soldier Palmer on the dropper, also No. 8. Excellent. Should I change down? The night was darkening as ten o'clock approached. A fourth and a fifth pluck made me gnash my teeth. By this time my hostess, who had had to attend a dinner party in the earlier part of the evening arrived and when she heard of the series of plucks remarked 'Ah, the prelude'.

I was weary of the this 'prelude' experience. I wanted to hook fish, so I changed my tail fly for a Dunkeld demon, about an inch and a half long. Fish were splashing all up and down the pool and some were showing more quietly on the margin of the far shore, a good twenty yard cast away. I lengthened line and first cast hooked a sea trout which played hard and threw out the hooks (I'll swear it was the demon) as I drew the fish over the net. Next cast another took, fled across the pool towards me, and threw the hook. If I had been gnashing my teeth before with five plucks I was swearing into the dark now with two light takes.

A third take felt quite different, A heavy pull and a boil in the still water below me and the fish was off. This felt very powerful, but ran like a salmon. It took thirty yards twice and then began wallowing, making great waves over the pool in the dark. It wallowed into a group of rocks and cut my cast through like gossamer. I could have wept. It was the first firm take of the evening. Time, ten-forty; light, getting on for pitch dark; drizzle intermittent.

I felt lost without my demon, but a dark Cahill No. 8 took its place. The Palmer was still safely on the bob. In five minutes I had a splendidly solid take to the dropper, three pounds nine ounces. I moved to the tail of the pool and made it a brace with a three and a quarter pounder. Shortly afterwards, after a splendid party in the dark, I took a fish of five pounds ten ounces. No more plucking, no more short takes. All these fish chose the dropper, took it well and were really soundly hooked.

The time was now eleven-fifteen and the first doldrums of the night started. Have you noticed this tendency of night fishing to have a burst, then a pause, and if your luck is in, another burst and another pause? Why? We might well try to answer that. At any rate it was close on midnight when I came back up from the tail of the pool to the middle stand and began casting. On this water, by agreement we finished at midnight. I made my last cast at about four minutes past as my hostess walked up the bank saying that we might be as well to call it a night. As she spoke I had a really solid pull and found myself playing the heaviest fish of the evening, slow, powerful, fierce, but with it all, unimaginative. It felt like being tied to a fat sow, rather than the tiger so often likened to the sea trout.

We had to put the light on to net this one, and when we saw it we realised that the sea trout net just wouldn't take it. It looked vast. It was either the best bottle of sherry we have ever hooked or a very respectable salmon. It turned out to be a salmon (13½lb.) and just got enough of its length into the big landing net to be brought ashore. On a ten foot Ivens rod (a rod I have killed an enormous weight of big sea trout and salmon on) it was quite a capture, even if it was a salmon. The interesting thing was, it too had taken the little Palmer, in absolutely pitch dark conditions. Most unusual.

Well, what does it add up to, apart from a night long to be remembered for its frustration turning to bad luck, then to what I call success? What changed, to our knowledge, during the critical two hours? Certainly the light faded from a deep grey dusk to a really fell black night. Further, the water which had been black after a small spate was clearing fairly rapidly after the fall and this process which I had noted earlier in the evening, no doubt continued. One important feature may well have been that the pool settled. Salmon which had been running up the river all day stopped running at night. Sea trout ran on through the dark hours, but I suspect disturbed the other sea trout less than salmon aggressively barging into the lies.

I think the demon precipitated at least two of the early losses. Demons are notorious for being easily shed. Fish which would pluck a smaller fly may take a demon and be lip hooked. I've noticed this often and I have in the past 'gone off' demons for this reason. I prefer tandems like the worm fly instead, but even they can unstick alarmingly under certain conditions of hooking. Probably time, coupled with deepening darkness, swung the balance. The fish which were stimulated to take the demon lightly would perhaps have been pluckers. The third loss was probably a salmon and should have come ashore. Bad luck smashing in these rocks. Thereafter the fish took a small fly (No. 8) the usual size for the pool, and they preferred the dropper, taking it firmly and well virtually on the bottom of a dark pool under a dark drizzling sky with no moon above. This feat of sea trout (and salmon), seeing a tiny morsel like a fly in total darkness is a marvellous thing.

And short rising? 'A prelude', said my hostess. Of course she was right. Regardless of what we think we are capable of in our fishing technique, there are times and places which must be absolutely right before sea trout will take properly. You may rush fish a little but the result will probably be lightly hooked ones. But, may I be forgiven for my language while I am waiting for conditions to change? Rationalising problems like this may be all right, but there never was a philosopher who could easily endure the toothache.

CHAPTER TWENTY-TWO

Wet Dapping for Sea Trout

The popularity of dapping for sea-trout is based on two principles, one good and one bad. It seems to me that when one takes away casting a fly from any form of fly-fishing, even if one replaces casting with another method of presentation, half the art of fly-fishing is lost, and with that loss goes the pleasure casting brings. I cannot believe that any skilled fly-fisher would, for instance, use a fly and bubble float with spinning tackle. Nor can I imagine any really keen fly-fisher for sea trout willingly giving up fly casting to dap, where a study of some of the problems of wet-fly presentation would bring sport which included the art of casting a fly.

But the dapper has clearly brought to light one of the main principles of sea trout fishing in lochs. The attractiveness of a dapping fly is that it can be fished in a irresistible bobbing fashion for a considerable time throughout the drift. The fly which presents itself at the surface, withdraws, and tantalisingly represents itself to bob on the surface is a known killer of sea trout. Dapping is found on this good principle and its successes leads to more consideration about the way of a sea trout with a fly.

It seems to me, however, that wet-fly fishing, properly tackled, can not only equal dapping in this attractive bobbing, but in one main way wet-fly work can outstrip dapping. I think of wet-fly fishing being a form of wet dapping, in which the bobbing fly is presented and withdrawn on the surface, not from above, but from below. It might be called inverted dapping.

The surface of a loch seen from below, as far as I can judge from my own experience of underwater swimming, or from films made by skin divers, is to a large extent a reflecting surface. The angles of the waves and the type of sky above, and of course the amount of wave affects the intensity of this mirror effect under the surface. A fly which cuts into this surface breaks the pattern. A dapping fly fished from above the surface cuts it from the air above and in bobbing disappears, or at least recedes into the air above the 'mirror'. The wet fly fished in an inverted dap, bobbing slowly up to the surface from below, with its hackles working, affects the mirror pattern from underneath.

The wet dap effect of a dropper on a wet-fly cast is without equal in loch sea trout fishing. One Brora angler of wide experience with whom I discussed this, called the essential idea of inverted dapping 'giving the fly that wet look'. This describes the surface bob fly as it appears bedraggled, cutting the surface before it is allowed to go back into the water again and open out its hackles and approach once more the underside of the surface.

Wet dapping with a conventional fly has added advantages. The fly works its hackles in the water beneath the top, works much slower than an aerial dap in its approaches to the surface and, probably most valuable of all, gives the sea trout a view of the fly in water, the fish's own element, whereas the aerial dap presents the sea trout with a fly from or in the alien air above the loch. This alone could account for the great number of fish missed by dapping from above.

Recently, however, I gave a full trial to a better dressing of wet sea trout fly. The idea, given to me by an experienced sea trout fisher, Niall Campbell, a man skilled in the knowledge of the fish, was to tie a conventional size 8 sea trout fly on a long shank low-water salmon iron of size 6. This idea is not new. Others have suggested something like it before. In this case, however, the theory was born out of the practical experiments that Mr Campbell had carried out on sea trout which rose short. I found the flies excellent, particularly in Black Pennell and Dunkeld dressings, tied up by Robertson, of Glasgow.

To present a wet fly effectively as a wet dap, it is essential to fish a long rod, and I had the good fortune to fish with two parabolic 12-footers which Charles McLaren, of Altnaharra, has designed for this type of fishing. He fishes them with light lines. I felt I had not the skill to use the No. 1 Kingfisher he recommended and I used an HCH (AFTM 6) Air Cel.

The advantage of having a long, swinging sea trout rod is that the bob fly can be controlled for a greater proportion of the cast than a shorter rod would allow. In addition, the offers can be better hooked , and usually more safely hooked because the sweetness of the 12 ft. rod bowing into the take of a good fish, places little strain on the cast and hook hold. It is, of course two-handed fishing, and for many this robs them of the pleasures of single-handed casting. I find the 12-footer slows me down and this alone, is, for me, a valuable effect. Instead of rapidly lifting line out of the loch to cast over a showing fish, I now fish out of the cast I am half-way through. So often the last yard of that cast brings an offer which an interrupted cast would have lost me.

In much of my own tackle, especially for trout fishing, lightness is at a premium in rod and reel design. I am not, I hope, being reactionary by re-discovering the delights of the longer sea-trout rod. I am adapting my tackle to a special need, which I would have thought every fisherman had to do in any branch of the art. The longer rods I fished were of cane. It may not prove impossible to design a glass rod to function similarly.

Perhaps, in my enthusiasm for the wet dap I have too readily condemned aerial dapping. To counter this impression, let me say that I believe that under certain circumstances aerial dapping can provide brisker sport with sea trout than the wet dap method of fly-fishing. Indeed, it can often be adapted to a form of wet dapping. For me, however, the wind is too fickle and uncontrollable a master. Casting a line is a pleasure I will not willingly give up.

CHAPTER TWENTY-THREE

Loch Sea Trout in the Dark

By general consent the sea trout is a wary fish, and by what
seems to be angling tradition is accepted as a fish not readily
caught in rivers by day but rising well to fly in the dusk and
dark. On lochs the sea trout is generally taken to be a day fish
and few have tried to fish them at night, and most anglers
accept the loch as hardly worth fishing after sunset.

In a recent very interesting correspondence I had with a
very experienced sea trout fisher I found myself looking back
over a number of sea trout seasons to bring together my own
evidence for or against the pattern of behaviour the majority
ascribe to the fish, and I believe the behaviour pattern is very
often a human one, not a sea trout one. Hotel and house party
organisation may play a bigger part in when we fish for sea
trout on lochs and may give rise to more of the general attitude
to night loch fishing than we would at first believe.

There is one small Highland loch well known to me on the
upper reaches of a small, spate river which I have fished several
times right through the night. It fishes well in the dark, and
like a river yields its biggest and best sea trout after sunset.
This little loch does fish by day, but less well than its stock
might seem to promise. I have always assumed that day fishing
here suffered from lack of wind and that this factor alone
prevented the loch equalling the bigger waters open to the
north-west where dapping and fishing large wet flies so often
brings really good bags of fish aboard.

We fish at night on lochs in summer in flat glassy calm
conditions – the very conditions which would make the day
fishing quite useless. Calm conditions at night have become
regarded by my little circle of night fishers as by far the best

111

for the loch I mention. We gently ease the boat round the drifts, casting out from either side with a two-fly offering. My favourite cast for this kind of fishing is a No. 12 tandem dressed Zulu, Worm Fly or Grouse and Claret. On the bob one could do worse than fish a No. 8 or 10 Dunkeld, Kate McLaren or any Pennell or Palmer. The astonishing thing on this water is the accuracy with which sea trout pick up the bob fly in pitch dark conditions.

I have known nights here when the floating line far outshone ordinary silk lines and I remember one evening when I had four fish running from eight pounds down to just below three, while my colleague, fishing a sinking line had no offers. The following season the sinking line outshone the floater although the floater did take a fair proportion of the fish.

Here then is a small Highland water, reedy at its margins, weedy in several places and nowhere more than ten or twelve feet deep. It fishes normally during the day provided the narrow glen with its steep sides allows enough wind to make a wave, and it fishes best through the night with excellent steady sport over its entire area.

I have also on occasions fished Loch Maree and Loch Hope until darkness set in. On Maree we were drifting in the evening at Kinlochewe and sea trout were coming reasonably in the light wave, rising to No. 10 wet flies. The average fish was around two pounds – not Maree at its most spectacular. Darkness fell and as the last light faded I lost a much larger sea trout. Then sport stopped – or at least, the last few drifts down the same water produced no more sea trout. We saw some tentative dimpling on the deeper water and on one occasion took two char by fishing these deep water rises. Having had a long day of it, and looking forward to the next day's sport, we turned for home after a short time with no sea trout rising.

On Loch Hope I was able to fish two of the beats over several occasions right into the dark. Again, like Maree, sport was consistent until the light faded, then with a last burst it stopped. This time, thinking on a remark Charles McLaren had made about sea trout at night in lochs I moved my drift. He maintained that night sea trout in a loch – the ones you would catch anyway – moved right into the margins of the water, even putting their backs out at the very edge. I moved to shallower water and cast in and took one fish. I saw in the glimmer of the late evening sky several other good fish moving, as Charles McLaren had said, right in on the stones. On one occasion I saw a fish moving between the shore weed and the dry land – probably in three inches of water. What slashing sport that would have brought if it had been tempted to my fly!

Just as on a river sea trout move position with the fading of the light, so on a loch they appear to do likewise. If we are to catch them we must follow them into shallower water. Notice, however, that my blank on Maree was a blank over the usual drifts, and my sport on Hope was achieved by moving into shallower water. On the little Highland loch I mentioned first of all there is shallow water all over it. Hope and Maree have a contrast between the twenty feet sea trout drifts of the daytime and the attractive shallows near the weeds and on the shingles which sea trout frequent in the night.

There is another factor which we should perhaps mention here accounting for the freedom with which sea trout on a loch rise by day while their kin in the rivers are virtually uncatchable by normal wet fly tactics – barring a spate with coloured water. The boat does not disturb sea trout. Fish which would not stir a fin in a river will rise right under the gunwale of the boat. In fact, it is close in that the really deadly work is done with the bob fly on a wet cast. Fish in a loch have also twenty feet of water, and vast extent of it, to give them a feeling of being secure. In a river, even a large river like the Sheil, there is always an insecure and limited cover for fish, compared with the spaciousness of the sea the sea trout have just left. Night comes on a river to blot out the terrifying land around. On a loch there is no such fear; it is one sea replacing another.

One of the few feelings of uneasiness I get in being a member of a house fishing party, or a guest in an hotel is that just when I am sitting down to my evening meal, and finding conversation and fellow-feeling becoming expansive, a really intelligent and socially ruthless angler would be launching his boat on the loch for the last burst of the day fishing and the indescribable mysteries of fishing in the dark. It is at times like these that I remember a night, long after midnight, when I had a strong take, my rod arched and a fish as yet only a sensation in the dark, tore line from my reel. Then, in a chance glimmer to the north-west shut in between black shadows of the glen sides, I saw the profile of my fish as it leapt – deep and short, cartwheeling and shattering the calm night surface of the loch with a great eruption. It came to the net eventually and weighed six pounds. With pictures like this in my mind I hope I may be forgiven if I seem not to hear the next lead in the conversation.

CHAPTER TWENTY-FOUR

Deep Line Fly Fishing: The Pleasures of Conversion

It is so easy to slip into a set way of fishing, especially when it is a sport-producing and aesthetically pleasing way of catching sea trout. I have had such sport with the floating fly line for sea trout that I have not only preached its merits and boasted its successes; I have also in the past become slightly biased against sinking the flies for sea trout.

There is one water I look forward to fishing on several days each year, the Endrick – the main feeder of Loch Lomond. There I fish a pool which has a superb stock of fish and its sea trout are perhaps the finest of their type that I have ever had the luck to cast a fly over. 'Over' is the operative word, since for the first season or two of my acquaintance with this water I always fished these sea trout with a floating fly line. I took occasional fish, often earlier in the evening rather than later in the night. My hostess, Mrs Elspeth Mitchell, knowing her pool far better than any guest, pulled my leg mercilessly about the tiddlers I caught by this 'sophisticated' method. Finally one evening, over dinner, she converted me. I agreed to try the untypical method of sinking my flies very deeply and fishing a small fly very close to the bottom in the dark.

I chose a Wet Cel sinking line HCH and a cast with a No. 10 Dunkeld on the tail and I began casting near the tail of the pool. I hooked my first fish in the grey dusk and it was a whopper. It fought like a salmon rather than a sea trout stopping to tug fiercely at the cast then running short and powerfully for short distances. Anyway my new 9 ft. 6 in.

Stillwater rod was well bent for several minutes before the hooks tore out.

I had hardly time to feel sad about this when I had two offers in quick succession and then a splendid take which produced after a sparkling fight, a four and half pound sea trout, clean and fresh and fighting to the net. I moved a little nearer the tail of the pool and took a three pounder almost at once. Again a nice fish which had positively engulfed the tiny No. 10 Dunkeld fishing slowly, very slowly near the pool bottom in darkness.

The best fish of the night came within twenty minutes. It took in a deceptively simple and gentle way near my bank and fought like a fairly light fish for some time until I decided I didn't need any help to land it and began moving the fish in firmly in the dark towards my net. Then I knew its full power. The fish fought dourly and hard and tried to slash at the cast with its tail. Finally with my little hand lamp held in my teeth and my net already in the water I saw the fish and almost gasped my lamp into the river. I was lucky to net it on the second time round. It bagged the net out in a most satisfying way and gave me once again the unforgettable feeling of staggering up a riverbank with one's net ponderously sagging in front, full of good fish. It weighed six pounds exactly.

If all teachers could reinforce their lessons with success like this there would be no educational problem. I had broken a fairly long tradition of my own by abandoning the floating line for one night. It had indubitably been the right thing to do and I should certainly not have done so had my hostess not argued so firmly for the tactics she knew would work in her own pool. It was a pleasure being converted – even for a night.

That was one of the milestones of my fishing career – and as subsequent seasons went on it proved to be a very significant beginning to a series of deep line experiments which have led me to the best sea trout of my life – fish of seven, eight and nine pounds in weight. Fishing deep line for sea trout has not, of course, been a panacea, for some waters do not yield sport to the technique. But it has often produced by far the heaviest sea trout of several seasons, usually fish in the four to nine pound class. In the chapters that follow I describe something of the techniques I use in this exciting method of taking bigger-than-average sea trout.

CHAPTER TWENTY-FIVE

Deep Line Fly Fishing: The Basic Techniques

There is more to night fishing for sea trout with a sunk line than merely, by hook or by crook, making your flies sink below the surface. I know of no branch of fly fishing that has made me think more carefully about the water conditions, the overhead conditions, the temperature and the light. Of course, we all think about these things whether we are sinking or not, but in no branch of the sport is vital environmental information more necessary for interpreting success and failure.

Usually I find myself interpreting *success*, for the sunk line in most of the water I fish in Scotland kills sea trout efficiently. In fast rocky water the line can't really get very far down, so the sunk line merely fishes mid-water like a silk line. In quieter water however, where there are stocks of sea trout available, a well sunk line with a normal night cast on will take fish well, often surprisingly well.

I readily agree that one of the pleasures of night fly fishing for sea trout is the sight of rising fish, and when the rise is seen to be to our flies our heart leaps for sheer excitement. But think back; how many times have you in fact seen a night rise to your flies? As I write this sentence in mid-summer I have just returned from a trip to the Border Esk where I had a dozen sea trout, taken at night, most of them on the floating line. I saw none of these fish rising to me, although in some cases I had seen the fish rising naturally seconds before I covered it and felt the pull. Night fishing is a kinesthetic skill, a tactile pleasure. The rod in your hands vibrates, twitches and bucks; the line between your fingers stops, tugs, tightens or 'goes heavy'. Night fishing could be practised, for the most part, blindfold. The odd fish one sees rising is an *added* pleasure, of course, and the night is thrillingly punctuated by splashing trout and Vee-shaped arrow wakes of big fish in pool tails. But I don't think we lose very much *visually* by sinking the night flies.

If we lose, it is rather the light sense of contact with the floating line and, particularly, with the flies as they search the top six inches of the pool's surface. Sunk line does bring a heavier feel to one's lining hand. I am reminded of one of my friends who drives a Mini Cooper criticising a multi-thousand pound saloon car. It was beautiful, he said, but too solid a feeling.

In my own fishing I find that the sensitivity of sunk line fishing is very much increased if one handlines the flies very, very slowly. One casts out the flies and lets the line sink, then, practically letting the fly settle on the bed of the pool, one *inches* the line back in. It is the nearest thing to legering a fly known to me. The sea trout usually takes the bob fly, but by no means always, and one presumes that it is gently moving up and down over the bed of the river, brushing against the noses of fish, or creating a very small aquatic disturbance which the sea trout sense in their lateral lines (their most sensitive detector) and become attracted. I once heard Eric Horsfall Turner say an interesting thing about this. For a sea trout to find a small fly, in a dark pool at night, it was similar to any one of us entering a totally dark room and being able to find a hot flat iron in the room with little error. I think sea trout do much better than us, but the principle is there. A sea trout feels its way towards your fly.

I remember a dawn on the Sheil in 1968 when I was fishing sunk line to end the night's fishing. I edged the fly gently, gently over the bed of the river, taking plenty of time and trouble over it, for I knew that the pool I was fishing (Garrison) held some very big sea trout. I wondered whether I was overdoing it, for the fly must surely be resting on the bed at times. A solid take dismissed these ideas and I found myself playing a fish of something between seven and eight pounds. It was a typical triumph of the sunk line, for floater had 'gone off' about an hour before. I played this fish for several minutes, checked its rushes eventually and survived its wild leaps, and

I began to lead it up to the grassy bank to land. But the fish turned and knitted itself three times through a ghastly bed of weeds at the top of the staging and nipped off my fly as neatly as you please. What a loss! Yet I remember this incident as a typical success of the sunk line. Weed is just a disastrous contingency which can rob you of a fish hooked by any means.

There are two ways in which the sunk line can extend the sport of night fishing in water where normally you would use floating line. Firstly, the sunk line can take fish in that lull in the night which I call the 'doldrums'. In Scots it would be the 'howdumdeid o' the night'. Then things quieten; fish rise less freely; the wind usually dies and many anglers go home. I remember, for example, on the Border Esk at Irvine House, taking a No. 6 Blue Charm from my box, attaching it to a sunk line and taking two fish from one pool in this non-productive time for floating line. On the Sheil I have often found sunk line very effective when the surface-fished fly or the high water fly was no longer raising fish in a pool like Captain's. A sunk line can therefore extend the taking time through the lull.

A sunk line, however, can help you to fish well on water which is regarded as unproductive to normal fly methods. I am thinking for example of the still dam pools we find on some of our rivers, of the slower moorland waters of Highland streams, and even of the little lochans that form on Scottish and Irish rivers between faster gravelly fishing. There the sunk line can search out the depths and can surprise you with what it takes. The finest example of such a pool known to me is the one we have already mentioned on the Endrick, Craigbel. This water was a mystery to me for more than two years. I could catch salmon on it and at night, fishing a floating line I could catch smallish sea trout, say under two pounds in weight. With persuasion, as we have recalled in a previous chapter, I took to sunk line on this pool and it not only opened up a marvellous piece of night sport, but brought me a quality of fish far and away better than floater ever produced there.

This question of better fish taking the sunk line is an interesting one. I have had my best sea trout to date on the sunk line, $9\frac{1}{2}$ lb., from the Endrick. But I have had three fish in the eight to nine pound class in recent years on floater on other waters.

It is really not only a question of sinking the line, as we stressed at the beginning of this chapter; it is a question of a group of variables, and these, critically, include the kind of bottom to the pool and the speed of the water.

The best bed for sunk line fishing at night with a fly for sea trout is either a sandy one or a silt one. Rocky water, where the rocks are still proud of the bed is confusing. The flies touch and stick, jerk free and, worst thing of all, blunt their points on the submerged stones. I have found certain parts of Highland rivers poor for night sunk lining for this reason, and the Doon, my home river in Ayrshire for many years, is virtually unfishable with sunk line for sea trout on all but its dams.

What kind of rod, line and cast should one choose for best night sunk lining? Be sure you choose a rod which has power reserve, for there are times when a big sea trout six or eight pounds in weight will take the fly from the bottom and suddenly charge to the surface and leap against the drowned line. The rod, which you involuntarily lift hard and bend into the leaping fish is subjected to great strains in such circumstances. A weak rod can snap at the ferrule. Only a cane of good making, such as the three models we recommend in the 'manifesto' (Chapter 19) will serve you well. Ten footers are best, if you can handle them easily, for length of rod can help you to roll line out of the water prior to re-casting.

I favour a slowly sinking line such as the 'Half-and-Half' Cortland or the Wet Cel 1 (the slow sinker). There are others too, equally effective. Some people do very well with an old worn silk line, say an old Kingfisher No. 3 whose dressing has more or less gone and when wet, the silk line goes down steadily, just like a slow sinker.

I have made myself a special sink-tip line for this work, especially in an attempt to counter the drowned line which can be such a menace with a big leaping fish. I have spliced two yards of wet cel (from a salmon line whose tapers I was tampering with) on to the end of a Gudebrod floater HCH. The effect is of the line riding high with a more or less steep gradient down the sunk tip from the surface to the flies. The idea – one much exploited by reservoir fishers for trout – works well and I would not be surprised to find the sink-tip taking fish just as effectively as the old sunk line, and saving me the odd moment of great anxiety because of drowning. There is also a good chance that a sink-tip such as I describe will work the flies very attractively. Where the sunk line lying on the silt might foul the flies in mud or weed and would tend to make them plough through the bottom greenery, the sink-tip would elevate the flies as each little retrieving impetus was imparted. But several seasons of work will confirm this. At the moment it is speculation.

I usually fish two flies for sea trout at night, whether I am fishing on top or deep, with a sunk line. The dropper fly, call it the 'bob' since it is usually fished within a yard of the line, takes many of my fish. Sunk line fish take the tail fly as often as they do the bob, but floating line fish show the reverse trend, more fish preferring the bob. I love a palmer-style bob fly, that is, a fly with hackles wound round the body to form ranks of 'legs'. The hairly movement of the flies seems critical. Of all the patterns mentioned in this book as successful for sea trout I incline to the Dark Mackerel, a fly rather like the Mallard and Claret but with a gold rib and a gantron claret body. Only Dickson's of Edinburgh tie them. I believe it was invented there as a Loch Leven trout fly by Mr David Leslie. I find it a great night killer in the size Dickson's call No. 6. Most other tackle dealers call this No. 8. Dickson's use Martin's 'outpoint' hooks and they can hardly be faulted for strength, hooking powers and holding qualities.

A demon or a large tube fly often works very well on the tail of a sunk cast. I have had some lovely fish on a two inch Garry Dog salmon fly, bumped across the bed of a pool. What a take this sometimes brings! I can never forget the thud of two sea trout on the Boat pool on the Border Esk. In one case I was at the end of the pool and had moved nothing. Leaving a long line out I turned to move out of the pool and stumbled a bit in the dark. I paused to regain my footing and pick my way out and the line, still out, was sinking very deeply. Then I found the gravel and waded more briskly. The tube fly probably lay inert on the shingle and as I waded must have leapt up and started to swim for the shore in a determined manner. A fine fresh sea trout absolutely hammered at the fly and was very soundly hooked. On a previous outing another had nearly wrenched the rod from my hands in much the same position when I was fishing a tandem lure deep down. Takes of the large fly are often dramatic, but of the smaller fly are often hardly distinguishable from touching weed.

It is not everybody's idea of pleasure to fish sunk line. To some it is coarse; to others infuriating, for the bottom may be hooked too often for an unfrayed temper. To me it is tremendously exciting and a producer of 'bottle' fish. Yet, given the choice I would rather have a half hour on the floating line with three or four fish splashing at the flies than the same on sunk line with only tweaks to show the fish's takes. Usually, sunk line takes are solid and unambiguous events. If a fish is lost, it is lost during the fight. We all know that the floater is not like this. Fish may move to you, pluck at you and fail to take hold. We miss seeing the half-offers to the sunk line, and thus we miss some of the agony (and the pleasure) of the night's sport when the curtain of the surface intervenes between us and our four-foot deep flies. But sunk line fishing is above all a variation on the fly fishing theme, and it is a productive variation. That should earn any method a trial by a keen angler.

CHAPTER TWENTY-SIX

Deep Line Fly Fishing: Further Perspective on Big Sea Trout

I will place 1965 in my records as the finest year for big sea trout I have yet known. Oddly enough 1964 was my best previous year, but 1965 yielded to me and to my fishing companions several remarkable catches which I doubt if we will ever see bettered. I have already written in several places in this book about some of my techniques in fishing big sea trout at night and among the ways I have described has been the highly productive sunk line technique which I use on certain slower stretches of water with considerable success. Two recent results by friends fishing similar water make such striking proof of the case I have argued for sunk line that I think them worthy of consideration.

On August 24th I was invited to fish my favourite stretch of the Endrick again – that prolific little river flowing into Loch Lomond – and I was this time asked to bring a friend with me if I cared. I invited Oliver Williams whose successes with sea trout and a floating line on many waters in Scotland impress me. He is a splendid fly fisher and passionately keen on night fishing. I explained my view on fishing a very deeply sunk fly for sea trout on the Endrick and when we got to the water he reversed his Cortland 'half-and-half' line to fish the sinking end. Oddly enough I had chosen that same line for my fishing that season since the loss by theft of my delightful Wet Cel.

The night rise on the Endrick has usually two phases which the owner of the water describes picturesquely as 'the overture' and 'the rise'. This summer there has been a distinct lack of 'overture' and a very brilliant night rise, often late in the darkness. I had two fierce plucks during the overture just as light was fading. Oliver went over to the far side of the pool just before ten and I had the satisfaction of seeing him fast in a fish almost at once. After ten minutes I decided matters were serious and I crossed by the bridge to help him. The fish was heavy and dour at first then powerful and immensely strong in two runs. A chance glimpse by torchlight took our breath away. It was certainly the biggest fish we had ever taken at night.

It was twenty minutes before I took the fish in my net and staggered up the steep grassy bank with it. It was a huge cock sea trout exactly thirteen pounds in weight and solidly hooked on a No. 8 Wickham's Fancy – the dropper of Oliver's cast. What an 'overture'! From what I can gather this is the second biggest sea trout ever to come out of the Endrick, and in 1965 in Scotland was among the heaviest two or three fish taken anywhere in the country.

The overture was an hour and a half before the rise proper. It was eleven thirty before the fish began to take again but between 11.30 and about twenty minutes after midnight we took seven between us, all fish of the three to six pound class with the best of this batch a five and three quarter pound fish I took at the last moment before we stopped fishing. Total, eight sea trout to two rods in two hours, weighing 34½ lb.

Since then our hostess, Mrs Elspeth Mitchell, fishing alone had a catch of nine sea trout in the dark between nine in the evening and midnight. These nine weighed no less than 38½ lb. and in 1966 she bettered this with a catch of eleven sea trout and one grilse, weighing 43½ lb! On both nights she stopped fishing with the fish still rising well, completely satisfied with the fantastic night she had had.

But let's have a word of caution here about our sunk line fishing. I spent a fortnight fishing the Doon and Stinchar in Ayrshire and found that the sunk line would not work *at all*. All the fish came to the floater. These fish however were small sea trout. Again, fishing on a large still pool on the Moidart, two friends of mine, infected by my accounts of sunk line sea trout fishing, fished sunk line all night and caught nothing while I switched back to a floater and killed four. Again, they were large fish, the best eight pounds.

Clearly my findings are somewhat contradictory in this. If

it is the pool configuration that dictates the conditions under which sunk line sea trout fishing excels the Moidart tends to disprove it. If it is the size of the sea trout that makes sunk line fishing worth while, again the Moidart argues against it. I have also caught heavy fish with the floater on other west highland rivers.

I have a suggestion to make which may put some of this into perspective however. All my floater fish have been either very fresh, or comparatively small, say under three and a half pounds. Most of the larger fish I have taken by sunk line methods have been fish in freshwater for, say, a week or more, and some in the Endrick seem to have spent some time in the loch before running up the tributary. Nevertheless, I have a hunch that even in a community of staler sea trout the freshest or the most recent arrivals in a pool are the keen takers.

A small feature of tackle emerges when you have some hard work to do with a sea trout rod. I have been fishing in recent seasons a T. C. Ivens 'Lake' a powerful 10 ft. cane rod and I long for an extension butt. When the fish is being brought in to the net one tends to hold the butt hard into one's body and this can (although it has not yet done so) jam the reel handle against one's jacket or waterproof coat. I insist on single handed casting however for night fishing. Line acceleration is invaluable for the high back cast which saves snagging on fences, bushes or rocks. I regard the worst fate of night fishing to clip the point off a hook in casting and lose a fish as a result. I may say it is a kind of therapeutic nightmare, since it makes me cast High Line/High Speed style and I have not as far as I can remember actually lost any fish through point breakage at night.

CHAPTER TWENTY-SEVEN

Sensitivity and Sea Trout

It is not often a fisherman prays for low water and quiet, calm weather. When he does it is likely that he is going to fish sea trout in the dark. A friend and I had two consecutive July nights recently on the Nith and Esk when conditions were strikingly in contrast, and when bags of sea trout told their own story. Our night on the Nith was unforgettable if only for the frightful rain and wind we encountered as we crossed the Dalveen pass. We arrived to find the river drumly with an inch or two of fresh water. Sea trout showed in the pools and we fished them hard for several hours. The brownies in the river were stimulated by the water and the conditions and we caught several good specimens of these, but the sea trout resolutely resisted all our lures and sent us home on that windy wet night empty handed.

We were in despair because the Esk date was the following night and we left Edinburgh in conditions of high wind. We noticed a change as soon as we passed Hawick, however, and by the time we had woven our sinuous way through Eskdale we found sheltered conditions, ten degrees warmer air, midges dancing in the shade of trees and, in short the ideal still, warm conditions we looked for to bring sea trout sport. Best of all, the pools were well stocked.

At that time I fished all my sea trout in river and loch with a floating line. I did this for several good reasons. Firstly I like to be in control of where and how my flies are fishing, I like to be able to detect the least twitch of a take in the dark, and perhaps most of all, I like to be able to make a riser show himself in the deep dusk and give me some indication of what kind of fish he is and his speed. All these advantages the floating line gives you.

On our Esk visit however, I found that the brown floating line I began with lacked one thing, line visibility. It fished well for late daylight fishing, but disappeared in the dusk on the dark still glides of the pool tails where the sea trout were sporting in the gloom. In addition the eleven-foot rod I had started with was tiring me. I found I wanted a more sensitive rod for the dark. Accordingly, I changed to a light green floater fished on a nine-foot-six rod and thereafter I was in control of my sport with hand and eye.

We took thirteen fish between us and I attributed many of these well hooked fish to the ease with which I could see my green floating line against the dark glassy surface of the pools. But even with the green line there came a time of night when the fish went off. We took no fish between half past midnight and half past two. Any countryman will tell you that the earlier time is late evening and the later time is early morning. One could sense this by the waterside. Bats were still fluttering at twelve thirty; a solitary bird sang for the dawn at quarter to three.

Did I say we took nothing in the doldrums of the night? Forgive me. There was that two pounder which taught yet again the lesson that sensitivity of tackle is essential for night sea trout. I was longing for the dawn rise and had started down a gliding stream when I felt an almost intangible something happening to the line. It was like a tiny temporary weighting, just as if a wet stick had brushed against the cast. I tightened and was into a fish which fought very hard in the dark. It was a two pounder firmly hooked in the root of the tail. Any angler knows how hard that fish must have fought. I am sure I had raised the fish to my flies and equally sure that it had not taken. It had touched the cast however with its back as it glided past the fly. Because of the sensitivity of the floating line and the lightness of the little rod I had felt this and in striking, had foul-hooked the fish.

If you meet the kind of angler who fishes his heavy salmon tackle for sea trout at night because the fish can't see it, tell him he is wasting his fishing time. A sea trout is as delicate a feeder as any fish I know. He is less guarded at night than

Above: Fly fishing a pond near Edinburgh. Pond trout fishing has a quality all its own and many anglers have developed good fisheries in small, but productive waters like the one shown. The angler is Richard Connel of Edinburgh. *Below:* Fly fishing the Hoddom Castle water of the Annan. Michael Shepley fishing

Above: Wet fly fishing for trout on the Leaderfoot beat of the Tweed.
Below: Playing a sea trout on the flats below Captains on the River Sheil. The angler is Mr R. O. M. Williams who knows the sea trout fishings of the Sheil very well

during the day, but he is not an abandoned fish. A floating line is one of the ways to treat a sea trout as he ought to be treated. It is also one of the ways to hook sea trout as they ought to be hooked.

When a sea trout rises at night he might splash at the flies, (this is whitling behaviour) he might head-and-tail over the cast or under the flies, or he might merely suck in the flies making little more than a swirl on the top as he moves. With a sunk line the splasher might be hooked automatically, and with luck the head-and-tailer might have the hook pulled home as you lift the line for the strike. Equally, lifting the line might pull out the hook. The dimpling or gently taking sea trout will not even be suspected on a sunk line. But on a floater the gentlest take communicates.

So when we pray for stillness and low water we say something about our whole approach to sea trout. We want gentle conditions in which to use sensitive tackle, and above all, we think the sea trout is a wary fish worthy of fine treatment.

CHAPTER TWENTY-EIGHT

Scratching the Surface of a Sea Trout Loch

How do you behave in the fortnight or so preceding an important invitation to fish first class water? If you are like me, you will find yourself carefully following the weather charts, incessantly asking people who have passed through the area of the Highlands you are to fish to describe the conditions. If you are lucky enough to have a friend fishing the water before you, you often make long and expensive calls to ask in detail what the fishing proved to be like in the conditions he found. In short, I become what educationists would call 'highly motivated'. Those who live with me often call it by another name.

In August I was to fish Loch Eilt, a splendid West Highland sea trout loch, which according to my fifth column reports, was better stocked than for many a year and was returning bags as good as any of recent seasons. With good news like this in my ears, I watched the weather settle, knowing it to be the best state for this particular loch.

Two nights before I drove north it began to rain. It was the first real rain for weeks. I was depressed. To make matters worse several of my close fishing friends started to ring me up excitedly saying that the rain was going to give us all unforgettable fishing. They could hardly agree with my groans of complaint since they were all going to fish rivers with grilse runs and these waters undoubtedly fish superbly just after an August flood. I think there were several rumours about my sanity at this time. I was marked out as the man who groaned when a summer flood came.

I duly arrived at the twisting glen road that leads down by the lochside to Lochailort and saw that the loch was some two feet higher than I had heard in my last report. It looked marvellous and the wave it carried went a long way to dispelling the theoretically based depression I had carried for some days since the rains came. The waves lapped against the roots of the old pines on several of the islands, early heather was blooming and the waterside stones shone grey beside them. The loch looked and said 'Fish' in the way waters assert things to highly motivated anglers.

The first day brought calm conditions with some quite spectacular bands of mist hanging between the braes of the lochside hills. The hill feeders roared at us, filling the already high loch with more warm water from the hills, as we idled down our best drift near the shore. We picked up small fish, herling and sea trout of up to a pound and a quarter. Twice in a half-hearted puff of wind we began rising good fish to both wet fly and dap although the rising was only a fraction of the activity my host had seen earlier in the week before the water rose.

The pattern of the rising gripped me. The fish would move apparently quite slowly to the fly, swirl at it boldly at the end of the approach and, I'll swear, never opened their mouths to the wet fly at all. When it became possible to dap a little during the afternoon, the fish would hardly move at all to the surface dancing fly. In terms of failure (to be Irish) wet fly failed better than the dap since it failed to hook more fish!

The next day again started calm but set a fair wind to help us by about eleven in the forenoon. With this wind fish began to move better and we had two sea trout take the dap firmly in our first drift. Neither was big, but each one was well over a pound and fresh. Finnock came fiercely at the wet flies we offered and many were returned, but the better sea trout which in this water run well into the 'teens of pounds were not to be tempted. Occasionally they moved to the dap or to the well worked bob of the wet fly, but in each case the fish 'came short' and those that we were able to see rising near the boat were popping up through the waves at the dap with their mouths firmly shut.

Throughout both days with my host, his ghillie and I discussed the sudden change in the fishing and the feelings I had had originally about the fishings were substantiated. The findings of our boat at least ran something like this. We agreed that the sea trout were there and that on the second day at least the wind was right. Thus, the first contrast we established was between the first day of little wind (and little fish movement) and the second day of reasonable wind and better fish activity. The bags for the two days were comparable, however. Both were low. Wind may have affected how many fish we moved, but wind did not seem to be the factor influencing their taking the fly. Water height was more or less constant, since the loch was emptying as fast as the still active hill burns filled it.

But there was one vital factor which had dogged both days – a factor which I believe is the key to all good loch fishing, for brown trout or sea trout. It can be stated in two ways, either as a surface layer of water on the loch which is radically warmer than the top sub-surface, or, stated in terms of oxygen, as a surface layer of the loch which is less rich in oxygen than the wind whipped surface of a Highland loch might be expected to be.

All the best sea trout lochs of Scotland are well blown by the northwest wind. These lochs dap well and also yield good bags to large wet flies fished jauntily on or through the surface. They are best in steady weather with steady medium winds for the simple reason that this allows the top two feet or so of the loch to become both colder than the water immediately below that layer, and better oxygenated by the wave action and by the ability of the top water when it cools in the wind to dissolve more oxygen.

To relate this story of dissolved oxygen to the fishing it is only necessary to think how characteristically lively a fish is in colder, well oxygenated water and how sluggish a fish becomes in still conditions in warm weather. Sea trout especially are not shallow water fish in the way salmon and brown trout are. You may raise your best sea trout from twenty or thirty feet of water. If the fish comes from the colder depths to a warmer layer of 'stuffy' water it is likely to slow down, lose the urge to take the fly, and although it may still turn at the fly, it does not want to engulf it. More strikingly, it does not want to leap from the water to chase a dapping fly. Thus in flattish conditions of warm surface water the sea trout will turn at a wet fly and will not take a dap at all even if you do manage to make the light breeze lift your floss silk line out.

Of course my friends all had marvellous sport with their grilse on nearby rivers. There the rains brought comparatively well oxygenated water, and more important, brought fresh wild fish into the pools. They caught double figures of grilse in a day because of the spate which reduced our sea trout loch fishing to a very poor level. In warm days with settled weather and puffy white clouds like wigged judges in the sky, the loch fisher for sea trout fills his bag and the tenant of the nearby river catches very little indeed. What is hard to do is to convince some anglers that the loch and the river fish well at different times for exactly the same reason.

Explaining your failures in fishing may become a sport in itself, yet it is a pursuit which distinguishes fishing from the mass of other sports. Fishing impinges on the world of chemistry, biology and geology – to name only three areas of enquiry which we reach when we scratch the surface of our sport. My two days on that fascinating west Highland loch are in no way to be compared to two bad days at golf. They were two days of the most gripping fishing I have ever had. What's that you are quoting? 'Hieronymo's mad againe.'

CHAPTER TWENTY-NINE

A New Fly for Sea Trout

When we get down to thinking seriously about it, there is really very little we know about the way a fish takes a fly. This is nowhere more true than in sea trout fishing. Sea trout have made a name for themselves as short risers and most anglers are pleased to hook one out of three offers to the fly. On dap, of course, where the misses are really often apparent miscalculations on the part of the fish rather than normal short rises as many as ten rises to one fish hooked may be recorded.

If we accept short rising as a common phenomenon, however, it does not mean that we are not greatly irritated by it. Many anglers have tried to alter their techniques to meet the problem. Some have tried very rapid striking, others have delayed the strike until the fish has had time to turn away with its lip held hook. Some have tried the very short rod, say eight foot six, to be in closer contact with the fly; others have gone over to the twelve foot rod to have more control over the bob fly of the cast as it emerges from the water. But there is really very little in the way of specially designed flies for sea trout, to counteract this frustrating short take.

I discussed this perennial problem with Mr Niall Campbell one spring recently. He is at once a biologist and an angler, and as a West Highlander he has spent a great deal of time fishing for sea trout. He suggested a simple design of fly to beat the short riser, which I have now given a season's trial and have found strikingly successful under certain conditions.

Basically the idea is a simple one. A normal sea trout pattern in No. 8 size is dressed on to a long shanked low water salmon iron No. 6. Thus behind the sea trout fly there is almost half an inch of projecting hook shank. It is an obvious enough thing to do, to dress a fly like this, but in the years I have fished sea trout, I do not remember any attempt at all to try out the idea. Mr Angus Robertson of Wellington Street, Glasgow had a range of these flies specially tied up for me in obvious sea trout patterns like Black Pennell, Soldier Palmer, Connemara Black and Blue Zulu. With a leaf of my fly box filled with these elongated flies I could not help thinking as I looked at them, of a flight of herons trailing their legs out behind them in their slipstreams.

In the summer I tried these flies out on the River Shiel, Loch Stack, Loch Hope, the Kyle of Sutherland and several other smaller and less noted waters. On the lochs at least there seems to be no doubt at all of the superiority of the design. They hooked more fish than other wet flies fished at the same time from the same boat, generally outclassed other boats and on at least two occasions far outstripped the dap as a killer of sea trout.

On two drifts on Loch Hope I raised and hooked five sea trout without any miss. True, on an over enthusiastic re-run of the same water I raised two fish and missed them, but I believe this was in part due to my own stupidity, re-drifting water already disturbed.

On the rivers in which I tried these flies I had little success to report. On the Sheil the fish would not take them at all since the basic size I was fishing appeared to be above the size required. The sea trout there wanted something as small as a No. 10 and as I had no modified dressings in this size the experiment went by the board. We were fishing our rivers largely by night anyway and the short rising phenomenon did not seem to be very prominent. Fish took sincerely and well when they bothered to come at all.

The significant thing about the flies however, was the way they hooked the sea trout. Most of my fish this summer were hooked in the roof of the mouth about midway back, and not in the angle of the jaw. This seems to suggest that the fish took the fly itself (I mean the actual dressing) in a hold very far forward in the mouth and in making a sharp turn away with it, were hooked by the projecting long shanked hook. A normal fly would either hand pulled out of the forward part of the mouths of the sea trout with only a vague pluck to indicate the take or at best would have taken a precarious lip hold only.

There is one other factor which might confuse the issue however. I was fishing a twelve foot rod on the larger lochs that year for sea trout. With this longer rod I worked the bob fly for a much longer distance over the water than a shorter rod would have allowed and most of the takes I had came at this point in the fishing out of the cast. I suggest that the hooks themselves, however, made the position of the hooking secure, even if the longer rod made the actual strike easier.

I regard this year's sea trout fishing with these flies as a mere beginning. It will take the opinions of many experienced fishers after wide trials to determine whether in fact the design has gone some way towards hooking the infuriating short rising sea trout. As I write this, however, I am quite convinced that they made my summer sport far better than it would otherwise have been.

CHAPTER THIRTY

The Olives of the Spring

I was fishing for salmon on a beat of the Tay in late March near the confluence with the Tunnel at Balinluig and as the day warmed up to a half hearted mildness around one o'clock my attention was taken off the salmon fishing by an amazing rise of trout. All over the pools they rose and from the boat when we were harling our baits for spring salmon we could look with the light and see the March trout as they fed furiously on a splendid hatch of flies. At that time we had not had an offer from a salmon and I well remember cursing myself for not bringing my trout tackle out with me. Trout well over the pound mark were splashing at every fly that floated down. The trout were obviously dry fly fish offering sport of first order to a large floater. In the middle of this splendid piece of activity when my mind was certainly not on the doubtful pleasures of harling for salmon in spring a fish took and trout vanished from my mind as I bent the rod into the first springer of the day.

Later that day the salmon tenants from the beat below brought in a big brown trout which had taken one of their harled spoons. It was dark, but not lean, and weighed something over two and a half pounds. Later in that same week a friend of mine who knows the Tummel well was fishing below Pitlochry and among the excellent fish he took on fly was a trout of four pounds.

For years I have been preaching to fellow anglers not to fish for trout too early in the season. Parliamentary law might say that we can fish for trout in mid-March, I would sermonise, but trout are in no fit condition to take until mid-April. Well, publicly, I recant. What I should have said was that the Tay system probably yields its best trout fishing between mid-March and mid-April. After that, the fish rise less freely, are much more wary all round and are, in short, difficult fish.

What is it that makes Tay – a cold river by any standards – fish so well in March? Without doubt it is that fly that in entomological ignorance Scots call the Dark Olive. On the dark surface of the salmon pools of Tay, sometimes in snow flurries, sometimes in rain, the large dark olive hatches and flutters its saturnine wings. Watch a hatch taking place and you can see a fly emerge and perch on the moving surface like a black rigged ship. Watch it carefully. It sails along, goes round into a slightly slacker reach of stream where the pool deepens and 'Plop!' up comes a March trout to engulf it.

The large Dark Olive is easy to identify, because it is often the only fly on the water in mid-March. In really cold weather the fly emerges such a dark drab olive that it is sometimes described by anglers as a black fly. In fact the male is a darker fly than the female. Harris in that indispensable angler's book *An Angler's Entomology* described the Male Dark Olive (*Baetis rhodani*) . . . 'Their bodies are a dark, drab olive or olive-grey and between the wings the upper surface of their thoraces are a dull grey or bluish grey'. The female has more of the typical yellowish olive in her colour. My impression is that in March the flies I examine all seem (most improbably) to be males. Temperature is on the angler's side usually in mid-March. It is seldom mild enough to make the hatched dark olive duns fly off quickly. Instead they ride steadily down with the current for long periods after hatching and make excellent sitting meals for feeding trout. But you can fish to imitate these hatching dark olives by using wet fly or dry fly, since the floating flies so prominent on the surface were themselves only minutes previously nymphs struggling out of their shucks at the surface as they hatched into duns.

Many anglers fish large Blue Duns as an imitation of the Large Dark Olive. Some find that a large Dark Greenwell fills the bill. I have very pleasant memories of fishing a quill-dressed version of the Dark Olive so big (No. 10) that it would not float for long and taking trout after trout. Indeed one angler asked me once to bring him back from Edinburgh a dozen of this tying before the spring went any further.

One of my friends who fishes early for trout on several of the Border streams believes that the finest imitation of the wet (nymph) Dark Olive is the Woodcock and Harelug with a twist of gold at the tail. This is a fly I have never had success with. My friend however fishes gaily with a large wet Hare Lug No. 10 or, if the day is very cold, No. 8 and he takes good baskets of trout when other anglers with smaller flies are doing nothing. He tied a Dark Greenwell for early trouting which has the darkest starling wing he can procure. It lies nearly black on the palm of the hand and reminds one of night flies we have used in midsummer for trout. These big patterns are well worth a trial in the opening weeks of the trout season when Dark Olives are about.

I took very misleading advice about early trout fishing when I was a beginner. I was led to believe that dry fly only paid off as a spring technique when the air and water had heated up sufficiently for many species of fly to hatch. This may well be a true general rule, but March has virtually only one fly and it is an exception. I remember fishing the Doon in Ayrshire early in spring and finding dark olives scattered over the surface of the streams. My wet fly seemed capable only of taking salmon parr and in desperation I turned to dry fly and tied on, of all things, a large Parachute Grouse and Claret. I took a trout of over half a pound almost at once and shortly afterwards had a brace in the creel. Then in a surprising burst of activity I found myself hooking, not trout, but sea trout kelts which seemed to be in a shoal in this particular pool. I spent an hour with my trout rod bucking and bending into these kelts before the day darkened and the rise stopped.

In the first week of April on the Spey when I was fishing a delectable beat for salmon I saw a rise of trout then of sea trout kelts just like the original experience on the Doon. I stopped salmon fishing for half an hour and, fishing wet, again had a brisk battle with some well mended kelts which seemed none the worse for their experiences, before the rise suddenly stopped and I turned again to the more serious business of tempting spring salmon.

Of course, don't quote me to your irate host if he comes up to the best salmon pool in March or April and finds you 'wasting time' with trout. Some tenants of expensive salmon beats have the odd idea that their guests should be productive! I know of one case where an angler pointed out to the ghillie that there was a splendid rise of trout to Olives and suggested that he be put ashore to set up his trout tackle. The suggestion fell like heresy on the ears of the faithful. 'Trout rather than salmon!' It was an indictment of insanity.

Look for the dark olives, then, on the cold, unwelcoming waters of March. Look for the fly in snow showers in that 'blinky' kind of day when pitch black clouds alternate with a hard patch of blue sky. Fish for the first trout of the spring wet or dry, preferably in gentle streams and in sheltered places, and expect about an hour and a half's brisk sport around lunch time. Make the most of it. *Baetis rhodani* comes and goes like a whim in mid-March.

CHAPTER THIRTY-ONE

Hot Summer Evening on a Highland Loch

After the end of May the beat I fish on the lower-middle Tay falls off somewhat and for a few weeks it becomes a gamble whether the grilse and sea trout will be there to provide sport or not. In a good year the springers hold on well providing sport right into the middle of June and they are quickly followed by shoals of grilse which give excellent sport with the fly. In late May one year recently in the middle of the first real Whitsun weather we had seen for some time in Scotland I had a message from a friend of mine who has the fishings on a Highland loch on the upper reaches of a salmon river. Would I come and fish for trout, he asked, adding that there were some salmon showing in the loch too.

I jumped at the chance, disposed of my rod on the Tay and drove north on a brilliant sunny day which sent my fishing heart into my boots. The loch, stretching from the garden of my friend's house on its banks to the sweep of the hills on the far shore, lay like glass. Birch flies (a sure sign that summer is really here) whined round us. It was more like swimming weather than fishing, but my friend who has made a special study of his water in all conditions over a number of years insisted that we would catch fish.

The interesting thing was that even in the first drifts in the middle of the afternoon we found co-operative trout. The fish were picking up a number of types of fly, including several clearly off the heather, and we had four good fish in an hour – the best one pound one ounce. But this was only the prelude to the excellent surge of activity we were to find after supper when the trout rose with some determination.

On our first drift in the evening my host took me to a long snag-filled shallow where the river entered the loch. Two or three salmon showed splashily round the branches of trees brought down by recent spates. Trees on a drift like this can be a great hazard, but they can also be very useful drift and lie markers. In this case I used the menacing twigs of one tree branch as a marker which helped me to cover a few square yards of shingle lie beneath it with great care.

I was fishing a new ten-foot trout rod I had just had sent up from Sealey's, the *Maxfly* – a rod with a double-built butt but the most delightful action which brings out the fighting qualities of trout as well as anything heavier you might get into on a Scottish loch. We turned over a trout or two, mainly fish moving to a small worm fly No. 12 on the tail of a three fly cast. At the tree I fished carefully round the side of the branches, finishing with a rather daring cast right across the back of the snag, hoping that I would not foul any underwater twigs. My line stopped and I took up the strain gently. A strong pull saved me the trouble of setting the hook. There was a boil on the surface followed by a small splash. I was into a salmon on a trout cast in positively the worse lie for snags on the whole loch.

Anglers who have played salmon from boats on a loch will know that they fall into two classes – the tigers and the lambs. This one began like a lamb and followed the boat as we rowed hard to get away from the obstruction, and also to take the struggling fish away from what might be a lie worth fishing again in the later evening. I was careful not to get the fish on to the reel in the early stages of the fight with light tackle. The clicking of the reel seems to annoy salmon I have found, and I always handline, or clamp the line carefully to the rod butt when I want to 'walk up' with a fish. This time it worked like a charm. The fish followed the boat docilely, and indeed at one point was only about ten feet behind and below us and with my polaroids I was able to see it swimming along in an unagitated way as if oblivious of danger.

The tone of the fight changed when we reached open water and stopped rowing. The fish moved firmly and then made a series of vicious rushes which at one point ended in a superb cartwheeling leap which took our breath away. It was a splendidly fresh fish, very deep and in our excited estimation might run into the lower teens.

As the salmon began to tire (quicker than you might imagine on trout tackle) the question of getting him into the boat arose. The fish was on the tail fly which gave it fully nine feet of cast to work on. My rod was well arched with the strain of moving the fish (thank heaven for the double built butt!) but it became clear that we would not get the fish steadied on the surface beside the boat as things were because of the cast length and the danger of the cast knot jamming in the top rod ring. I decided to add height to my position and, against all my instincts and all my advice to other anglers, I stood up on the seats of the boat, with one foot on the stern seat and one on the rear rowing one. I suppose I was safe enough, even if rather bizarre looking, but please don't anyone try to imitate me! It did the trick though, and my host expertly gaffed the fish and lifted it aboard. What a beauty! Thick and fresh, although not as heavy as the spectacular leap had made us think. Nine pounds, but perfect.

I would heartily recommend anglers who fish for trout on highland lochs where there is a chance of a salmon in summer, to use a ten-foot rod. A rod like the Sealey combines sensitivity with reserves of power and there are times when you thank your stars for these resources. I have been a keen 'butt action' man for some seasons and I have had several salmon in rivers and several really heavy sea trout too on two rods of this design, but there is a stage at the end of the fight when a salmon has to be moved carefully to a netting or gaffing position and the supple butt of the 'butt action' rod does not make this any easier. Further, I would say that the rod with the stronger butt was less fatiguing to fish with for long periods.

The day I describe finished in the long, late dusk of the evening with a rise of trout coming on in absolutely still conditions to that little heather beetle which we imitate with the cochy bondhu (or the small worm fly). These were superb trout feeding in about six inches to a foot of water hard by the heather and grass of the bank. We took trout about, one gently rowing the boat along the margin and the other casting to rises or searching the likely water. The first fish was just under a pound; then came a trout of one pound five, and a second one of a pound and a quarter. Six trout in all were netted in three-quarters of an hour and several were lost. It was trout fishing at its best on a Highland loch.

I preach a lot about when to enjoy Highland trouting at its best, but what distresses me most about visitors is that they fish during the day and after dinner tell each other fishing stories. Why not tell the stories during the day and fish from dinner till midnight? The bag will be doubled in size and probably will be of an average weight which few would have thought the loch capable of producing.

CHAPTER THIRTY-TWO

Light on Fly Fishing

In trout and salmon fishing alike, we so often look down into the water we are going to fish and gain an impression of the light conditions which are based on a human eye looking into water rather than a fishy eye looking out of water. If this is not imposing the limitations of the angler on the sport, I believe nothing is. What a fish sees above it in a loch or river is often a very different thing indeed from what an angler sees looking in.

On a bright day, glare off water is most noticed by us if the boat is drifting into the sun. But below the surface the trout which is moving steadily into the wind has the sun on his tail and actually gains a very great advantage from the light behind. Under such conditions fishing can be good. It is almost always true to say that when the opposite conditions prevail sport will be non-existent. The trout which is faced by the sun shining from the eye of the wind will not see your flies, indeed, will probably not be willing even to swim in the upper layers of the loch at all because of the discomfort of moving into a hard glare.

On a river the stream and sun can combine to give hopeless conditions if the sun shines down the pool, and often a good sun shining upstream, particularly if it is a low sun, can give excellent sport.

I remember having a good bag of trout on the Girvan one July Saturday when other anglers had given up because of the sun. I looked for a stretch of water where the sun shone upstream and fishing a small dry fly on light tackle, I found the trout keen to rise. On several salmon rivers I have walked miles to get to a pool before the sun would get round to a certain angle and spoil the light for me. Once on the Thurso I waited for over an hour near a pool until the sun moved off it and the first run down the water produced two pulls, and later two fish, unfortunately kelts. Even the kelts teach us something. In this case it was that the sun and stream must part company if the fly is to be seen properly by fish.

In Lapland my companions and I had an interesting problem with the midnight sun one July. When the red light shone flatly down the river fish would not rise. Given twenty minutes and a slight change of angle, however, the trout and grayling again rose and fishing progressed briskly.

The sky above the water is a vital factor in judging how a fish sees the light. A clear sky gives the surface a hard glittering mirror-like effect from below. A soft grey sky gives a ground glass effect. If you have ever looked for flighting duck or geese at night you will know that the sky which is hard and clear gives the worst possible conditions for seeing the birds. The diffused moonlight over a thin ten tenths cloud brings up the silhouettes of birds remarkably and even small duck can be seen clearly. So with fish the diffused light is the best one.

Evening light is a difficult thing to judge when one is either trout or salmon fishing. I have seen a loch boiling with rises as fish scooped in nymphs from the top six inches of water and yet one's flies were repeatedly missed by trout when they were presented. It may be that flies fished *on* the surface have a different optical environment from flies fished a few inches down into the loch. It may simply be in those cases however, that our flies do not interest the trout in the proper way and the rise is not really a take at all.

In spring several of my friends fishing greased line on Tweed, and Dee have reported salmon taking the fly late in the evening – much later than was normally thought usual for the time of year and place being fished. In one case a salmon was hooked on a tiny tube fly at ten o-clock on a May evening and it was landed in the dark by torches. I have often thought that the last ten minutes of daylight has a charm about it which fish seem to like. It is a time when a moist evening air gathers and wind dies away. On salmon rivers, pools which have had splashing fish all day grow quiet and somehow purposeful. In this light the fly is often of fresh interest to the fish.

One question I often ask myself is 'How in all the world can a fish see a fly in poor light?' Even in darkness when the rod you are holding is out of sight trout will still see an ordinary trout fly. Sea trout, of course, are legendary takers of the night fly and I have seen fish shying away from a fly in deep dusk, but taking a very much smaller fly in darkness proper. The answer to how the fish can see such a morsel in such low light is perhaps to be found by turning your own eyes up to the sky above the river. On a summer evening you can see sometimes in darkness, bats in flight, silhouetted against the grey sky. I have even seen beetles and moths when one crossed my line of vision. You cannot *look for* things like that. It is only when an object crosses your most advantageous line of vision (usually to the side of your eye at night) that they are seen. So it is with fish. Your fly cuts across a sea trout's sensitive area against the sky and up he comes to take the mite firmly.

Light is a vital factor in all forms of fly fishing, but it is a factor we cannot judge clinically. We can try to think like a fish and we can apply our findings. Often they work; but in the final analysis it is really a kind of metaphorical way of thinking. We hope our judgement in one sphere applies in another. We should perhaps take courage at times from the exception to the rule. One ghillie told me that in conditions of bright sun with the light right down a pool he once took two salmon on a tiny Thunder and Lightning. One angler writing in a fishing magazine some years ago swore that he prayed for bright sun downstream to give him cover, in the dazzle as it were, to approach big trout in a quiet pool. And, sadly, so often the light is just right and trout will not believe it and will not rise well. If only someone could throw light on that problem!

CHAPTER THIRTY-THREE

Climate and Micro-Climate

The gamefisher's year is governed by broad cyclic developments as the season progresses. The spring salmon arrive, the first trout rise to our flies, the sea trout show in our rivers and lochs and grilse shoals are noted arriving at the height of summer. So it goes on in broad movements, year after year. But the general cycles of things are not the crucial factors for anglers who have to take their fishing when their fixed holiday comes round or more delicate still, who have to select in advance days on good water, which depend on rain, wind and temperature rather than the broad trends of the season for their sport. Summer fishing is critically governed by these lesser features of the gamefisher's year.

I was once given four day's fishing over a fortnight on a little Ross-shire river in the last two weeks of July. I first saw the river in drought and found myself wondering where the tales had sprung from about this being a salmon and sea trout beat. I could walk across it at a dozen places without wetting my shoes. Midway up the beat a much lauded waterfall and falls pool was a puny trickle down a green rock face.

But the weather changed. It rained. It was not a torrent of rain, but one wet day followed by a topping up of a shower or two. The little river became a medium sized river with attractive salmon pools and long sea trout flats. The blank days of the first week were succeeded by two of the finest days of sea trout and salmon fishing I have had. And as the flood subsided the evening sea trout fishing came into play and brought excellent sport.

That experience has been repeated for anglers so many times in Scotland in July that it is to be taken as a hoped-for pattern of summer fishing. In the changes that take place in a little summer flood, however, an angler has to adapt his fishing if he is to make the most of the splendid opportunities the spate brings.

I should hate to sound a pessimist, but it is a fact that July rain, especially if it is of a thundery nature, is often very cold. This means that the flood it produces may well lower the temperature of the river considerably, often into the forties fahrenheit. Fish are significantly affected by this drop and salmon may well prefer a large fly fished well down in the flood. I have taken fish in late July and early August on 2/0 flies in floods on the Naver, Brora and Thurso. In all cases the salmon the day before the flood were demanding trout sized flies or at best, low water dressings of very small salmon flies. Don't jump to the conclusion that there is a one-to-one relationship between fly size and water height. In fact my experience suggests that there is a closer relationship between size and temperature than size and water height.

In terms of water colour and fly fishing I would not like to generalise. Let me recount a summer experience on the Awe in which I went very wrong in extraordinary conditions of water colour. I found the river at normal height but very muddy indeed because of excavations of the river bed for the new hydro dam. I decided to fish large flies regardless of water temperature, since I thought the salmon would never see a small fly in such turgid conditions. Across from me, the 'opposition', a local angler, began fishing greased line and low water flies. He killed one fish almost at once and followed this with a fine sea trout a moment later. What was his fly? A No. 6 low water Lady Caroline. The difference between the floods mentioned earlier on the northern rivers and the flood (simulated) on the Awe was that the former were cold floods and the latter was a warm one.

Really, it is not climate that the gamefisher is interested in, but micro-climate. He is interested in the temperature of a water at a given place, on a given day for instance. In terms of micro-climate an angler in summer is also interested in how the wind strikes the water at a special place too. I remember fishing Loch Leven at the Sluices end and an east wind with a haar cut down the summer temperatures we predicted to something less than was comfortable. The fish were clearly affected. Only a few trout fed in the open water but the main feeding activity was along a shore where the lee of trees made a micro-climate several degrees warmer than the open water air temperature. There the trout massed and fed brilliantly on hatching midges. We saw fifty or sixty in one drift. How many did we catch? None. We could not tempt the fish on this occasion because of the 'anglers' curse' of midges. With another type of fly hatching we would have filled the boat.

Micro-climate can be large enough to cover a whole parish or small enough to cover the square foot behind a stone. My favourite example of the effect of tiny variations of wind causing extremely good fishing conditions in a small area is of wind on a pool or on a shallow boulder strewn loch bay, causing a 'slick' of foam to split round a protruding stone. Slicks are filled with trout food, drowned, drowning, hatched and hatching – a little macabre cameo of aquatic insect life. Trout take up positions in the spindrift behind such stones and are easy meat for the well placed fly. Charles McLaren of Altnaharra once told me laughingly that he and his brother, as boys, used to fight over who should fish a slick first because of the certainty of fish taking. There are all too few fishing certainties of this calibre.

As usual, it is the angler who has an eye for natural observation who makes the most of local conditions. There is no sport so dependent on chains of natural circumstances as fishing. Which way a thundercap breaks up, how the wind veers and what temperature the rain is are as important in their way as what flies are hatching, where the trout are feeding and how you cast your flies out. Really, all these factors are interlinked; some are natural phenomena and some (the actual angling part) are skills. Skills alone are virtually useless.

The problem of summer fishing, then, could be crystallised as the difference between a calendar and a diary. We book our holidays by the calendar, but the precise conditions we meet are diary entries made from experience of how the weather and the fish affect each other. I started, years ago, to keep a newspaper weather map for each day I went fishing, but I gave up the practice because what I found in a valley often contradicted what I would have found on a mountainside.

Twice I drove through July gales to the Nith, and Border Esk to find quiet conditions in a sheltered gorge. In each case the local conditions made or marred the fishing. Now I keep a 'weather eye open' in the original sense of the remark. I look to the wind (and the other elements) in a particular place and time, and, if I have the skill, I adapt my methods accordingly.

CHAPTER THIRTY-FOUR

Scottish Lochs: A General Survey

To think of the lochs of Scotland as one simple unit of the fishing of the British Isles is at best an over-simplification. At worst it is a highly misleading idea which could ruin a fishing holiday and disillusion anglers. Within its comparatively small land mass, Scotland has a great variety of fishing lochs – some very good, many without real distinction, and some downright poor. Probably the water chemistry of each is the only really safe way to classify these waters from an angler's point of view, but there is no readily available data on the vast majority of lochs. Thus one looks to the environment – the rocks and the soil – when one is classifying trout lochs. Interestingly, the key to loch sport is written in the stones.

Most experienced trout fishers are well aware that Scottish trout lochs are as varied a collection of fishing waters as might be imagined. They vary from the fishless and unfishable to some of the most rewarding and memorable fisheries in the land. Within the range of trout lochs there is what might loosely be called a hierarchy. Fitting an individual water into this hierarchy is of the greatest value in approaching its fishing with the right tackle, and probably more important, with the right outlook.

Coarsely I have found it useful to divide Scottish lochs into brown and green waters. Brown waters are affected by peat drainage or are themselves set over peat and the water takes on a brown tinge which may vary from a light sherry to strong tea in shade. While it is valueless to make generalisations about fishing from mere colour of water this can at least start an angler on the right chain of thought to make the most of his fishing. The more peat stain, broadly speaking, the more acidity; the more acidity, the less bone and body-building food. Thus a dark brown loch – often called a *dhu* loch in the Highlands – may actually be fishless. Other darkish lochs may have only a poor stock of small black fish.

It is not that trout grow more slowly in peaty water. This idea has now been clearly disproved by the research of Niall Campbell (The Growth of Brown Trout in Acid and Alkaline Waters. *Salmon & Trout Magazine No.* 161) in which he showed that given the right balance of stock, trout in a peaty loch will grow as fast as other fish and even faster. Usually peat lochs in the Highlands have far more fish than they can grow to good average weights. Thus hordes of quarter pounders often dominate. This position is aggravated by the good spawning so often available in hill lochs.

The green lochs of the Highlands are much less common than the brown ones. The greenness in the water is sometimes associated with limestone bedrock or shell impregnated boulder clay in some plains. These are usually well known fishing lochs with food supplies able to maintain a balance of pounders or even better. One discovers green lochs in odd places, some that are easy to account for and some hard. I know of one landowner who has a small plane and who spotted one of his own hill lochs from the air looking far greener than its brown neighbours. He investigated further and found a fishery of unsuspected quality near other lochs of little value.

The biggest significant area of Scotland in the general imagination is the Highlands. Vaguely, this means everything north and west of a line from Loch Lomond through Perth to Aberdeen. But within this area rocks and soil vary enormously and we must try to see other divisions. The first is to see the highlands above the Great Glen (the natural fault running from Fort William to Inverness) as a separate unit. They might be called the Northern Highlands and strewn among the low rugged hills of this area lie many thousands of trout lochs. Most are small and most are of the order of mildly acid water (pH 5.5–6.5) containing fish of half pound average at best and five to a pound average in the worst cases of over stocking and underfishing.

The Northern Highlands cannot be regarded as one simple region in itself, however. Basically it is a spine of ancient metamorphosed granite with an extraordinary west coast – outstanding for its scenery of fjords and mountains – and an eastern and northern coastal strip of Old Red Sandstone very different in scenery and character from the rugged west coast. The far north then is a kind of geological, and fishing sandwich. Orkney and Caithness and eastern Sutherland and Ross make up one slice, the rugged west coast from Cape Wrath to Skye makes up the other slice. In between lies the old hard rocks of Sutherland and Ross and Inverness. Without doubt, the finest trout lochs lie on the margins of the area.

Orkney and Caithness have many local 'sweet' soil overlays in their old red sandstone and lochs in this region have a reputation not only for fabulous individual trout, but for a high average weight of fish and, best of all, a rapid growth rate of fish. In Orkney where a pH of 7–8 is normal there are cases of a pound a year growth being noted. One seven pound trout was exactly seven years old. This is outstandingly good fishing potential. Loch Watten in Caithness has in its day averaged 1 lb. and has produced its regular two and three pounders. Today it is less good than it was, but under its new organisation, should attain again its peak. Around Caithness there are lochs of great quality, rich in trout food, and producing hard large fish of splendid shape and colour. The scenery is flat and peaty, but to many, possessed of an irresistible charm.

On the west coast of Sutherland and Ross there is a strip of country which is the best watered area of Europe. In Scourie parish alone there are upwards of 300 lochs, most of them fishable. Most are small peaty waters, but tiny local pockets of sweeter stone (such as limestone) produce individual waters of quite different character. The small peaty lochs of the north-west of Sutherland for instance, round Lochinver or Scourie, provide fishing with heavy baskets of smallish trout, but appearing in the baskets with frequency are fish of the two to four pound class. In several fishing trips to this area I have seldom missed seeing or catching trout of several pounds weight. Many of these great trout are lost since they are hooked on light tackle, but there is no doubt at all that the general average of about five to six ounces is not to be taken as the only size of fish the north-west lochs produce.

A band of limestone runs down this region from Durness

following an almost perfect north south line, but disappearing from time to time. On it around Durness are the famous Durness lochs noted for their very large trout, running to ten pounds on occasion. These are not trolling lochs which produce *ferox* type of trout, but rich trout waters running to mild alkalinity in their chemistry. Remember their names – Croispol, Calladale, Borley and Lanish – for there are few waters like them in Scotland.

The trout fishing of the outer Hebrides has earned a name for excellence, but this excellence is again to be analysed by soil and rock classification. Generally speaking the outer Hebrides are of ancient metamorphosed granite and normally such rock would produce mildly acid waters, as it does in the interior of Ross-shire and Inverness-shire, say. But the low lying Hebrides, swept by the Atlantic waves have large areas of machair – that is sandy low lying land where the soil is almost pure shell sand. This means that these lochs are over the chemical equivalent of chalk and the waters are rich in trout food. The trout of Uist for example are fat well marked fish of a pound average in many waters and well above this in some individual places. All the islands at some place have shell sand, and some of the northern Highlands also have this excellent exception to the peaty soils associated with granite. Barra, Tiree and on the mainland, Morar and Arisaig are areas with this excellent soil affecting its lochs.

Ordinary granite is scarce in Scotland, occurring mainly in the Cairngorms. It is not usually good country for lochs. Waters tend to be hard and cold and barren in granite country. This is the place for char and occasional large *ferox* but not usually good for anglers. Otherwise, in the bulk of the Northern Highlands and the Grampians (the Central Highlands south of the Great Glen) lochs fall into two main groups. One, the deep clear lochs, lacking in weeds and gravel and fly life. Trout are scarce in these hard clear lochs. Two, the shallower more peaty moorland lochs where trout are plentiful but seldom average more than half a pound. Thus, where lochs lie directly on the rocks of the Highlands they tend to be barren, but where there is some soil, even peat, a better trout environment is formed. Examples of fairly poor trout lochs in this region are Loch Tay, Loch Earn and Loch Ericht, while many of the nearby lochs of Rannoch Moor are shallow and comparatively productive.

Skye and Mull and part of Argyllshire near Loch Awe are volcanic in origin. Fishing in these areas is often outstandingly good as a result. Mull has its Mishnish Lochs, Frisa and smaller waters, all examples of clear lochs which, at their best produce trout of well above half a pound on average. Frisa and the Mishnish lochs are in something of a decline at present, but have been splendid in the recent past. Igneous rock is often a pointer to good trouting. Bands of the volcanic rock appear in central Scotland and Northern Ireland. Renfrewshire and North Ayrshire have many of their more successful reservoir fishings over it and the few lochs of the Ochill hills in Perthshire are over the same good base.

Loch Leven is the water it is because of its rich alluvial soil, left by glaciers in the last ice age. It is a shallow green loch of pH 7 rising towards 8 as the algae mounts in summer. In many ways it is an exception – a kind of English water fortuitously set in Scotland. Its fish average a pound, when in condition, and good bags are taken from May onwards. At the moment this loch is scarcely living up to its name, but there are hopes that the decline is only temporary.

In the Lowlands of Scotland, over the coal measures, there are few natural lochs. Reservoirs have been made in many places, however, and these often produce splendid fishing. Coal measures are, of course, limestone, and the top soil in these areas is often very rich. Ayrshire has good loch environments in its rich agricultural land, but here again, reservoir fishing is largely the order of the day. Edinburgh lies near an area of trout ponds and reservoirs, many of which benefit from contact with carboniferous limestone and the rich loamy soils so often associated with it.

There are few lochs in the Borders, but again reservoir fishing among the rolling grassy hills can be of high quality. It is a far better region for rivers and burns. The western half of the Southern Uplands however consists of Silurian rocks mainly – rocks which are far older than their neighbouring coal measures and new sandstones. This band of Silurian rocks runs over to Ireland and is found also in central Wales. Over this type of stone, waters tend to be acid. There are more lochs on its surface than in neighbouring areas, and the trout tend to be prolific, rather like the Highland trout over metamorphosed granite, but the average does not often cross half a pound. Again, look for exceptions to this rule. Patches of rich alluvial soil in valleys may hold trout waters of much better calibre and coastal lochs are often perched on limestone patches.

What is the summary of our rock interpretation of trout lochs? Basically that the lump of Scotland, the Central and Northern Highlands do not produce good trout lochs when the waters are over bedrock, and over peat produce trout fishing of quantity rather than quality. Down both eastern and western fringes of the north however, there is exceptionally good fishing, usually associated with limestone bands or overlays. The Hebrides score where they have shell sand, producing some of the finest trout water in the country. Lowland waters are scarcer than Highland by the nature of the land but carboniferous limestone with good top soil produces good reservoir fishing. Igneous rock in Lowland and Highland areas outstrips granite. The Southern Uplands, made up largely of Silurian rock is rather like the Highland metamorphosed granite in that, characteristically, it produces quantity with only middling quality of trout. In all areas however, local alluvial soil or shell sand or pockets of limestone can produce top class fishing apparently exceptional for its locality.

CHAPTER THIRTY-FIVE

The Ascent to the Red Loch

Each season I try to make it my business to explore one or two hill lochs that I have heard about, but through lack of time or sheer laziness, have not climbed to and fished. I like to imagine that up there, over the first or second ridge, lapping the granite and heather, lie waters which are far more truly Scottish than the lochs to which one can drive one's car, launch the boat and drift where thousands have drifted before. In this way climbing to a small hill water is a spiritual as well as a sporting exercise. With the Red Loch it was no exception. Body and soul went through the hoops.

In western Inverness-shire, where the skyline changes from smooth glaciated curves to rocky, hummocky hills with knolls like carbuncles and where great petrified masses of boiling stone mark the summits, there are innumerable hill lochs trapped in corries or insinuated between the ridges. At altitudes of a thousand feet and over in this spectacular, hard country there is little vegetation and the lochs themselves, little affected by peat, lie clear and sweet over stony bays, and lapping low cliff faces. These waters are ideal environments for trout and, as we were to find out on our exploratory trip, their trout are handsome and large, and in some waters like the Red Loch are plentiful, to boot.

We travelled by car up to the head of the little spate river in the glen, called on the owner of the estate and had a chat about the fishing and were directed on to the best general line to tackle the wall of the glen, which looked impenetrable. Climbing, or rather scrambling, with fishing tackle to impede one is a difficult job. There is always the chance of a fall and a broken rod, and it pays to study how best to handle the rod on the hill. I recommend that it be carried loose in the hand and if one slips, it can be thrown clear. Rods tied through the fishing bag can take the full weight of one's body if there is a tumble.

It took just over an hour to reach the top of the ridge. We had five long pauses on the climb, during which we looked back and saw the glen and its tracery of burns extending map-like behind us. Lochs in the hills opposite began to appear as silver sheets and finally the big loch in the next valley revealed itself, sliding slowly out of concealment like a secret thing. From about eight hundred feet above the glen floor we had left behind us, the little loch on the course of the river seemed set out like a plate. A boat drifted on it and two anglers with dapping rods fished. Up and down the water white flecks marked the splashy rises of sea trout which we could see quite plainly from our perch on the glen wall. One almost had the impulse to call down to the anglers that a good fish had moved ten yards to the right of their boat.

We steered for the single blasted tree that marked the way to the Red Loch and within ten minutes the waters of the nearest bay appeared. In another ten we had mounted our rods, divided our ways, one to the left and one to the right, and had started to fish.

For a dozen casts there was delicious, highly charged uncertainty. I was using a floating line and a cast of wet flies and I expected to see every fish which moved to me, but the first offer was a sullen boil to the flies, and when I re-cast, the fish boiled again without taking. Before I could feel disappointed a trout of some three-quarters of a pound engulfed the Black Pennell on the bob and was played and netted. For a hill loch, this was a good start.

I worked my way down to a bay at the head where a rocky headland divided two likely reaches of water and here I moved one small trout which fortunately did not hook itself and immediately afterwards I rose a fish of what appeared to be salmon size. It swirled at my cast and showed a flank which seemed to be six inches thick. I have still burning in my mind's eye the sight of that flash of brownish yellow, and I still feel clearly the sense of emptiness in my rod hand when nothing at all touched my flies. I cast again and again, but the fish did not come any more. So the Red Loch was one of these waters, where one might reasonably hope for a two-pounder or, if I was to believe my eyes, a fish of double that size.

The next fish was just over the pound mark and the one which followed was only slightly smaller. What sport! These trout fought splendidly in the clear water, pulled hard and leapt daringly. In between missing rises and returning fish which did not reach the half-pound limit I had set myself I could see my friend's rod bending into fish and from time to time the waters in front of him opened up as a fish leapt and scuttered on the surface in the fight.

We had only three hours available for the day on the Red Loch, partly because we had sea trout fishing arranged for the evening, and partly because we had had a longish lie that day after an all night session at sea trout the evening before. With about three-quarters of an hour to go before leaving we each had four fish in our bag, and each had caught and returned many smaller. Both of us had hooked and lost good trout or raised and missed good fish. It had been brisk sport. But the last half hour or so was to prove quite amazing.

It began with the spectacular capture and equally spectacular loss of a big trout. My friend hooked the fish and I left my bay to hurry round to his side and take a few pictures. The trout fought dourly rather than well but eventually after careful handling came in to the net and was carried ashore. My friend took out the hook, praising the little Peter Ross which the fish had taken and lifting his landing net he banged the fish's head several times on the shaft to kill it. During the process it disgorged a newt. This provided some immediate interest and offered a clue on the diet of the big trout of the water. Since his hands were by now rather messy, my friend laid the trout down on the heather and wiped his hands on a tuft. I prepared to take another picture. It was a beautiful trout fully 2 lb. 2 oz. That picture was never taken however, since the 'dead' trout suddenly leapt into life, cartwheeled down the bank, hit the shallow water with a splash and, righting itself quickly in the water swam off into the loch! I ought to have photographed the look on my friend's face, but I suffered from a similar astonishment paralysis. Caught, and lost in the same twenty seconds. Robbed! Fooled! Yet we had one of the best authenticated losses of our career with plenty of film to prove our misfortune.

Whether the loss unnerved us or the lowering, weeping cloud which had suddenly enveloped us changed our luck, I do not know, but we discovered fish hard to hook after that. I lost three fish of the pound and a half class right at the edge. I also began in that grey, misty world to have fisherman's delusions. On one occasion I rose what seemed to be a very large trout but I missed it. I re-cast and the fish took. I landed it and found it weighed barely a pound. Had I lost it I would have sworn it was at least three times this weight!

We finished up with ten trout weighing 9 lb. 10 oz. which would do any of the fat lochs of the Lowlands credit. But what is twice the prize, we had found them in a little hill top water lying above a thousand feet up. We had fished them from water little disturbed by the legless anglers who would rather fish from the hotel window. It had been an exhausting climb but a splendid prize, and well worth the exertion; for experiences it was a day second to none.

We met the sea trout anglers from the loch we had watched from our perch on the way up. From the mass of splashing fish they had only had the luck to hook two and only to land one. No angler ever gloats over his sport does he? Shall we say we were merely glowing with that sense of well-being which comes from a stimulating hill walk coupled with three hours' fishing of the most unforgettable Scottish sort. The Red Loch will not be forgotten, and we will, we hope, meet its equal again in our hill fishing in the Highlands.

CHAPTER THIRTY-SIX

A Finer Approach to Scottish Trout

Scottish trout fishing is responsible for the making of many bad fishing habits. It is so easy in some cases that it encourages a slovenly approach to what, in other waters, is a very crafty fish indeed. Further, our stocks are so prolific, even if composed of small fish, that an angler who does not really care about his way of presenting a fly can still take a respectable bag of trout in many conditions. When bags are light, of course, Scots – and anybody else for that matter – can blame that greatest scapegoat of all, the weather.

Trout fishing in summer in low water conditions, in rivers where there may be a lowish stock of fish, is a sport which would defy all but the most skilful angler to succeed in it. It would make all but the finest tackle look coarse and it would break the heart of all but the most dedicated fisher. In summer I often find the lowly trout making me feel exceedingly humble, and making me think again about the skills I use in my fishing and the tackle I select to carry out my methods. A number of basic points strike one almost at once when sport has failed to succeed.

Have you ever thought that the end of a modern floating fly line was far too thick? I have and I have modified two of my fly lines to make the presentation of the cast much better. In both cases I was using C belly double taper floating fly lines which, apart from the criticism I offer, have served me well in every way in my fishing. To counteract the thick end I devised a taper in nylon monofilament which served its purpose well. I took a darning needle and bored it up the hollow core of the fly line at its very tip. I then brought the needle out through the side of the line about half an inch up from the tip. It was comparatively easy to thread a piece of 12 lb. nylon up through the core of the line and bring it out of the puncture in the sidewall. This was then tied in a simple whipped knot (like a four turn half blood) which jammed the end of the heavy nylon and left a perfectly smooth knot. About nine inches of this heavy nylon was left protruding from the centre of the tip of the line. One could then step down the nylon in any formula of taper one cared to use. I stuck to the Ritz tapers and found I could produce a dry fly or a wet fly cast which unrolled beautifully in presentation.

This modification has a very good side effect. You no longer lose little by little the fine end of your tapered fly line. There is no need to cut the line from one year's end to the next. You merely replace your nylon links. I found the taper both aesthetically and functionally more pleasing, and fishing a difficult little clear stream like the Haddington Tyne, I found presentation very accurate and results never better.

One of the refinements good trout fishing demands is in how the artificial fly is thinned out from its bushy shop dressing to a good representation of the fly on the water. Most shop-tied flies err on the side of over-dressing. But how do you thin out such a delicate morsel as a dry fly? Most certainly, you do *not* use scissors. Scissors are either-or tools. Feathers which are cut off have a block-ended appearance which totally destroys the natural tapers you find on fly antennae on fly legs and tails. Natural hackles have natural tapers, too. To cut them is to ruin the appearance of the fly completely. I thin out my hackles by a gentle stripping and plucking operation performed between my thumbnail and my forefinger. This is a selective method of reducing fibres, leaving many untouched and those it breaks it also tapers. The same effects can be obtained by using your front teeth, but you have less control over the operation that way than with your thumbnail, which you can at least watch as it works. Further, there is less chance of hooking yourself in the lip!

Manufacturers of fishing tackle are naturally interested in making anglers enjoy the tackle they buy when it is actually being fished. This seems to me to be one reason why so many manufacturers recommend lines for trout fly rods which are far too heavy for fine trouting. A heavy line makes casting easy, makes a rod work and is useful for distance casting and other operations. A lighter line takes much more skill to cast, but it produces a much more delicate result. I sometimes use an old silk Kingfisher No. 1 with a trout rod. It is really far too light to cast far but, greased, it fishes like gossamer. In modern fly lines I often drop a size against the manufacturer's recommendations, using on an 8 ft. 6 in. trout rod, for instance, a 5 floater (HDH) rather than a 6.

We are so used to fishing for trout with teams of wet flies in Scotland, three or four on one cast, that it is hard to think of a single wet fly being used extensively. It is *not* used extensively, but it is the answer when trout are shy, when waters are at low summer level and when one is obliged to fish carefully upstream, searching thin water with fine tackle. I have fished single midge nymphs on really fine tackle (1¾ lb. point) in this way and I have delighted in the accuracy it brought to my fishing. It raised some of the fishing near Edinburgh to levels of chalk stream skill (although hardly chalk stream quality of fish).

I find standard Loch Leven tackle alarmingly coarse at times. Three or four No. 12 flies on a six-pound cast is not an unusual specification for a Loch Leven fisher. The sad thing is, it works there. The standard advice is 'Fine tackle on Loch Leven is a waste of time.' A place with the prestige of Loch Leven, however, affects lots of the fishing round about. The cast you happen to have made up, for instance, is used on your local reservoir and if you have only two small trout for the evening, you blame the weather!

Scotland is too generous a tutor to make us learn really fine trouting techniques. Scottish waters are often tinted with peat and hide the defects of our tackle. Our rivers run with fast streams which disguise the shortcomings of our presentation and the quality of our flies. It is remarkable that the Scot has not already been totally corrupted by his environment and has ceased to fish in any skilful way at all. In fact the reverse is true. *Some* have been misled and are likely to mislead others, but the Scot is, generally speaking, an angler who wants to improve his sport, especially in the difficult conditions of summer. Perhaps the ways I mention represent how one angler, a hedonist looking for pleasure *and* results in fishing, has reacted to the more challenging trout of our summer waters.

CHAPTER THIRTY-SEVEN

Catching Big Pond Trout

A couple of seasons ago I was given a very interesting job to do for a local landowner. He had a delightful little loch of half an acre in which he reared brown trout and fished for them on summer evenings with a dry fly. It became clear however after new stock had been added, that there were still numbers of large trout from 2 lb. upwards surviving from previous stockings still in the pond and these were now going 'all head' and, in addition to indicating that the pond could not support all its fish under the new conditions, it suggested that the larger trout might even kill off, or wound the new stock of fish which were at time of fishing this water between half and three-quarters of a pound in weight.

Since there were small fish already in the water I was asked not to use bait and the task of fishing fly for the larger fish was given to me. It was stressed that I was to try not to fish for the smaller trout, if at all possible, since they represented the next season's table fish for the owner. I had therefore somehow, to attract mainly large trout – fish, I might say, which were as crafty as trout could be, having survived steady dry fly fishing for several seasons. In studying the problem, I re-discovered many things about trout – things which all too easily slip down into the well of memory.

I began by using conventional dry fly, a No. 16 Greenwell spider fished on 2 lb. nylon. This I used as a kind of survey fly, to find out if possible whether there was any area of the pond frequented by the new stock more than others. The Greenwell was seized with great zest by the new little fish and I was able to isolate two areas in which the little fish were shoaled in some numbers. The Greenwell did not take, nor as far as I am aware, did not even raise any big fish, in top trim, but this was expected. The big fish were not catchable on the first evening of my survey.

On that same first look at the pond I also tried to fix the time the big fish began to feed. Their style was at times unmistakable. They cruised in narrow channels in the Canadian pondweed and seemed to be very regular indeed in their habits. As far as I could judge, the big fish did not move until the sun began to dip and the air became still and moist in the summer evening dew. Then small rises, with strong 'plops' of noise would begin among the weeds and an occasional bow wave and a swirl would indicate a fish nymphing or perhaps even swirling at an intruding small trout.

That night I fished only dry fly, but the following evenings I experimented with nymphs of various patterns fished deeply sunk and on a floating line and greased cast, just under the surface. Several fish took the deep nymph, a No. 12 Claret Nymph with a mohair body, a silver rib and a sparse grouse hackle. It was actually a nymph I had tied up for loch nymph-ing and was based on the Grouse and Claret loch fly. This deeply fished nymph hooked three fish one evening and only landed one. The big trout took it when it was twitched after a long rest on or near the pond bottom and on feeling the hook each fish dashed into the nearest clump of pondweed and I was forced twice to handline gently but twice lost the fish by breakage. The third fish came out of its own accord, just as a pollack will leave seaweed if it is left to itself for a minute or two, and it was duly netted. The fish that took the nymph was a pound and three-quarters and rather black, although strong enough, in all conscience.

The late evening was the time for the really good trout to move. They began then to feed apparently on the surface, but as I discovered after several long and frustrating dry fly sorties, not actually on surface food. These trout were scooping nymphs from the surface film and a dry fly was not their meat at all. I discovered this by sheer laziness. The dry fly I was fishing was a Black Spider and I failed to oil it. It floated for a few casts and then began to soak and bog down in the still pond surface. I let it rest and soon I had a dry fly well settled in to the film. It was like float fishing for trout! I watched a crafty big fish scooping along on a beat which came within a foot of my fly and when he was about eighteen inches from the fly I twitched the rod top and the fly 'struggled'. He took with a beautiful suck, making a whirlpool on the calm pond. He was exactly two pounds and fought sluggishly, had a big head and should have made nearer three pounds in top trim.

The surface film was the place to fish in the darkening evening, but I found it was almost impossible to fish up to it by conventional nymphing. One had to fish down into it by letting the fly bog down. I soon discarded dry flies and used sparsely dressed wet flies, fished with a 'parachute' type of dressing so that they fell gently and settled down into the surface film. Then the merest movement when a trout cruised near almost always brought a take. But of all the fish in the pond I could not take anything bigger than 2 lb. 2 oz. although up to that weight I managed to hook a respectable number. I had been told to expect fish of up to four pounds. I can only say that I hooked fish with four pound length, or four pound sized mouths, but never four pounds of flesh on their bones.

During the operation I found out how important on a loch are the lines of feeding. Big trout beats once found were rigidly maintained, partly because of the weeds marking the routes, but partly, I'm sure, because the big fellows knew the richness of the food supply in these areas and were prepared to defend their beats against the smaller fish. I learned again that big trout will feed on the bottom as long as there is light enough to show them their bottom food. When the night begins to deepen they come up to pick out their food against the sky. Also, at dusk, winds drop and the still surface of the pond becomes oily and the static surface film presents a very difficult barrier indeed for ascending nymphs. In a slight ripple ascending nymphs can hatch and clear the water.

But out of all the fishing I learned the value of the twitch. The subtlest movement was all that was required to make the fly 'struggle' and to attract a cruising trout. Perhaps the most memorable lesson of all I re-learned was that big trout are nobody's fools. One had to think and work hard for every individual fish one rose.

CHAPTER THIRTY-EIGHT

Trouting on Eigg

Fifteen years ago, in an issue of the delightful but short-lived magazine *The Scottish Angler* an article appeared, 'The Delectable Island', by Donald Nicholas. It was a charming description, loch by loch of trout fishing on that remarkable capital of the Small Isles, Eigg. It was an article to make you want to follow the author's footsteps, for it described Eigg fishing in terms which made the adjective 'delectable' in the title seem insufficient. My chance to fish on Eigg came recently when a friend who now has a house on the island asked me to come and fish the lochs, since he and his family would like to gauge the quality of the fishing they offered. I was delighted to go, for I had often looked at Eigg from other islands, and like every observer had marvelled at the abrupt Sgurr, rising like the crown of a tall hat from the sea. In June of that year, one evening as I was setting out to fish the Moidart for sea trout in the dusk I saw Eigg through a notch in the hills of Kinlochmoidart. It was spectacularly bold against a pink sky. 'The Delectable Island' seemed to be waiting for me to sail to it.

I arrived on Eigg in Mediterranean weather at the beginning of August and my first sight of the lochs was under a sparkling sky. They looked gin clear and fishless. Urged by my host I cast a fly on three of the lochs and made some kind of fishing survey of each water. I raised nothing, saw no food at all, saw no rises and, I suppose, disappointed everyone greatly. I was not at all surprised. Hard bright sun never yet helped a loch fisher.

The lochs on Eigg nestle to the west of the Sgurr. Loch nam Ban Mora dominates the cluster. It is a splendid looking hill loch with an extensive area of shallows, a small stony island

and one or two deep holes towards the western end, near some small cliffs. There is a boat on Ban Mora, but it was being painted when I was there. I was happy enough to fish from the bank or by wading anyway. You learn more about a loch that way. Behind Ban Mora, to the northwest lies a very narrow boomerang of a loch called Loch Caol nam Cornbheinne. I swear you can see every stone on the bottom of this loch, and you would think no trout would live there. A few weeds offer some hope of food, but there seemed on the first day of viewing to be no shade at all. To the south lies a weedy loch shaped like a kidney (although one of the ladies of the party saw it as a heart) and promising trout, although nothing showed or stirred to our flies. On its banks however we found the largest trout skeleton I have ever seen. It was like a salmon kelt's bones. Alive that fish would have been five pounds or more. Other lochs dotted the high moor to the northwest, but in the heat of the first day we did not travel to them.

We had to wait in absolutely magnificent weather for four days until the cloud came down and gave us a soft Hebridean day. How different the lochs looked under a grey sky! I tied on a wet fly cast at Ban Mora, putting a No. 10 Soldier Palmer on the bob and a 12 Dunkeld on the tail with great hopes of fish. I still saw no natural rises, but the words of Nicholas's article came to mind: 'though loch nam Ban Mora can be dour, it can also be a dream for the dry fly fisherman.' I ignored the dry fly bit. I prefer to search out my Hebridean trout with a wet cast.

I fished down by the island, wading to the lip of knee boots, and near the tip of the stones I saw the waters of the loch bulge as a fish of some size swirled at the Palmer. Four casts later a fish came very splashily to the same fly and two casts later a trout took proper hold and I was into my first Eigg fish. It was a strong fast fish, clearly seen in the water. It leapt and showed deep yellow flanks and a scattering of spots I might have expected from a machair loch rather than a hill water. I called out to my host that I was into one, and soon slipped the net under him and took him ashore. It weighed a pound and three-quarters, and should I never see another trout, was the most beautiful of fish.

I fished a few casts further then reminded myself that I was surveying the group of lochs, not so much trying for a bag of Ban Mora fish. I walked over to Coal na Corn-bheinne, only a couple of hundred yards and there I raised several tiddlers before I spotted, as I was crossing a high bluff, a trout rising to dry fly. I recalled the terms of the original article, but I had a wet cast on. Even in the dead flat conditions there I cast out the flies. The trout turned in full view of me, and came several feet to take the tail fly. It leapt when it was hooked and played fast in full view of my perch. I beached it on the stones, a darker trout than my first but well shaped. It weighed fourteen ounces.

Having taken a sample from the boomerang loch I left it and moved over to the kidney shaped weedy loch, which I take it Nicholas in his article had described as 'a small loch with reeds in the middle just out of casting reach'. The weeds were all over the loch when I fished it and were very much *in* casting reach. Reeds themselves do not hinder fly fishing – in fact they can greatly help it by harbouring feeding trout. Weeds catch the fly and foul it however. We want none of them.

I cast out into the weeds and reeds where a small clear patch gave me a target. I handlined in steadily and my flies swam in clear view over water shallowing to under a foot deep. Behind my cast swam a large trout which brisked up his pace a little as the shore came near. What a fish! He made a sudden swirl at my dropper and missed. I whisked the flies out of the water and covered the trout again. This time he rose well and took the dropper. I tightened and felt the fish for a second or two before, in a great wallop shattering the still surface of the shallows he tore free and shot out to the weeds again, no doubt a wiser fish. That trout was perhaps three pounds. Certainly over two. It was a shame to raise it and fail to hook it properly. I never was certain of hooking fish rising to my dropper just under the rod tip.

The next nearest loch was one that Nicholas called 'The Breakfast Loch' since he could he said, guarantee a dozen or so six or seven ounce fish from it any day before breakfast. Optimist! I don't quibble about the numbers, but it would take two of these trout to make seven ounces today. I rose a trout first cast, second cast, fourth cast (without hooking one!) and finally took my 'scientific sample' after I had fished down the deep side past the sinister looking sunken boat beside the splendid weed bed. This loch, whose proper name in Gaelic is Lochan Nighean Doughaill – the little loch of the water horse – looks as though it could stock the entire island with fry. I would try a limited experiment on Eigg, taking a bucket with me to Lochan Nighean Doughaill and transporting half a dozen fingerlings at a time to Ban Mora and Kidney. A silver wire tag would be placed on each trout released. Ban Mora could certainly support more stock, and I suspect that the Kidney only has ten trout in it anyway, all huge.

We postponed the trip to several other little hill lochans and to one other principal loch, Lochan Ben Tighe. As usual postponement meant cancellation – at least on our first visit. I have fished the better half of the Eigg lochs, but others wait for another summer. One loch described by Nicholas as 'weedy' lay 'a hundred feet above Loch Kidney'. I couldn't find it. Two little weedy lochs a hundred feet above Nighean Doughaill may have been what he described, but I shall look again, more thoroughly.

What had my three samples fed on? It was a bag of trout of the greatest possible contrasts. A pound and three-quarters, fourteen ounces, but a darkish fish, and finally a small dark quarter-pounder. The big Ban Mora fish was stuffed full of caddis cases. The Caol na Corn-Bhienne (the boomerang) fish was full of what I would delicately call midge sludge. So was the Nighean Doughaill fish. The biggest fish was splendidly pink in flesh, the boomerang fish less so and the fingerling was white. I speculate on what the largest trout of all, the lost fish of Loch Kidney, would have fed on. I suspect it ate a trout a day, or a frog or two garnished with such other bottom food as it could find. Trout of this size do not live on flies.

Nicholas in the original article fifteen years ago said that Ban Mora could give half a dozen fish to two rods in an afternoon averaging just under the two pound mark. I believe him. I saw nothing smaller. His estimate of the average weight of Kidney fish was lower than I would believe. His weedy loch I have not fished. His 'breakfast fish' loch (Nighean Doughaill) is still a breakfast loch and my boomerang (Caol ne Cornbheinne) certainly lives up to his adjective 'good'. On one point he erred. He said that 'there are six or seven lochs which hold fierce fighting brown trout of up to four and five pounds'. These lay he said on a plateau 1,200 feet up with the most wonderful views of the mainland and nearby islands of Skye, Muck and Rhum. I say he erred. It is all true, but the lochs lie nearer six or eight hundred feet than he led us to believe. A description of a delectable island like Eigg had to exaggerate somewhere!

CHAPTER THIRTY-NINE

Some Personal Tastes in Tackle

There are two questions one might be asked about one's fishing: how one fishes for a certain species and why one adopts these methods. Between these two questions lies a great gulf. The how of the sport is a simple question of description, but the why involves us in questions of personal style which might be classified cynically as whim or, on more thought, be called questions of aesthetics. In asking a question about the why of one's style – putting oneself, as it were, on the couch, and there is every chance that some of the analysis will appear reactionary, even witless. Yet in this highly personal realm of the aesthetics of, say, sea trout fishing, lies the essence of the satisfaction of fishing.

In my bulky collection of rods and sundry gear, there is one excellent dapping rod and several boxes of dapping flies, yet in the course of a sea trout season I use these only as a last resort. There is something so highly unsatisfactory in the way a dapping rod is used – virtually immobile, like a flagstaff – that upsets me. The art is so much written on the wind and not in the tackle and the control of it that it seems to me to reduce the art of angling to its most passive, luck-ridden form. I realise that the minor adjustments one can make to fly behaviour in dapping are of subtle and, perhaps, vital significance, but as an art of fly fishing dapping robs us of casting, of swimming the flies, of that vitally important matter, contact with the fishing fly and this reduces it in my scale of fishing values.

Why then do I fish wet fly on the big sea trout lochs, choosing a long, supple 12 ft. cane rod? I dare say it is merely taste. I like the wet fly cast to begin fishing fast, almost as soon as the flies strike the water and, as it comes near the boat, I like to see my flies break into the surface film and, bob first, cut the furrow in the surface which gives a big No. 6 Black Pennell or Soldier Palmer what one of my Highland friends has called 'that wet look'. If you like, it is dapping from below the surface film. The bob fly moves up to the surface, cuts it, sinks back, rises again and cuts the film, and may even leave the water to flop back in again and 'wet dap' up to the surface.

With the long, soft rod and a line which the casting experts would say was inanely light for the rod (HCH, or even HDH) I am in control of my flies, particularly at the bobbing stage, in a way that neither the dapper nor the shorter rod would ever give me. It is a question of taste, really, and one fishes in this way for a complex range of reasons, but principal among these is the fact that this form of wet fly fishing keeps the flies near the surface of the loch and the movements of sea trout following the flies are often seen clearly, and at the bob stage their wild, and often abortive rises to the wet dapping bob are right under the rod top.

Certainly, this is a case of 'horses for courses'. This method is one best suited to really large Scottish lochs where there is usually a good wave. These waters have highly oxygenated surface layers and sea trout behave in them in a way they could not be expected to behave in other waters. Think of the principal Scottish waters and note, as an aside, how much in common they have. Hope, Stack, Maree, Eilt, Sheil and Lomond are all open to the northwest winds, are all long narrow reaches of water in glaciated valleys. Perhaps I can comfort myself in saying that my taste in tackle and style is a highly regional one, and that I am not really reactionary and anti-modern in my approach to sea trout tackle.

In loch fishing for trout, however, I find myself moving a little away from longer tackle but this is in itself due to my using floating lines on lochs almost on every occasion I fish. As far as I am concerned, the days of deeply sunk flies are over. What I find satisfactory in loch fishing is nymphing in the immediately sub-surface water 1 in. to 1 ft. down. I do, of course, on some waters (often waters with really large brown trout or rainbows) occasionally resort to a very deep form of nymphing, but for the rest of the season I insist on a floating line, a team of lightly tied wet flies and, above all else, a sensitive handlining technique which keeps me in touch with the flies at all stages of the retrieval.

Loch rods are still of the 10 ft. order in many parts of Scotland. Several main tackle dealers have emphasised this to me in analysing their customers. At least half of Scottish loch fishers would appear to demand 10 ft. rods and the other half spread themselves over other lengths from an extreme of 8 ft. to a popular 9 ft. 6 in. length. My own choice falls in the 8 ft. 6 in. to 9 ft. 6 in. range and I choose the rod I fish to suit the loch I will fish. Where waves are likely to be big, I like a long rod to exploit the bob action. Where waves run less, say on ponds and smaller reservoirs, I would take a shorter rod. But in this sphere, loch fishing, it is again a question of taste. Productively, a very deep fly might be better, but in terms of seeing the fish rise (and often miss), of being in finger-tip contact with the floating line and enjoying the surface fight of a good trout, the aesthetic pleasure of fishing light on a loch far outweigh the fishing with a single-handed ten-footer.

Sometimes in both trout fishing and sea trout fishing the main pleasure to be gained in fishing is to exploit a single sense in the technique. Dry fly fishing always seems to me a superb exploitation of the visual in fishing and the unforgettable and never stale rise to the fly is the key to the sport. In other forms of fishing, particularly in fishing for sea trout in the dark, the sense of touch or feeling is very highly stressed. I love using trout tackle for these sea trout. This is probably because the lighter rod of 9 ft. or just over throws a great deal more emphasis on the handlinings technique and it becomes a sensitive kind of communications game between the angler and the flies. The finger tip of the index of the right hand is the real focus of the sport. The line is drawn over this finger and, with experience, the subtlest differences in pressure can be interpreted. There is the soft drag of a strand of weed on the fly and one can even feel whether the hook point has become fouled by the weed because of the muffled feeling as the fly fishes in. Sea trout sometimes take with as gentle a pressure as the weeding of a fly. I remember fishing the Ross-shire Blackwater one night for sea trout and twice having the odd sensation that the weight of the flies had gone off the cast. In each case the effect was the take of a sea trout and the fish were duly hooked and landed. It was, if you like, similar to the method of tench fishing whereby the lifting of the bait from the bottom adds a leger short to the already critically cocked float and down it goes. To transfer all one's sensitivity to one finger tip is, perhaps, too sensuous a way to describe it, but sea trout fishing at night for me is often the exploitation of this feeling.

I am reminded, as I write about this question of personal taste in fishing method, of Pascal's argument about the pursuit of happiness by individuals. He held that men go to war for happiness, while others abstain from war for the same reasons. So it is in fishing. I might fish a long rod for pleasure; you might fish a short one for the same reason. The important thing is the reason. Even arguing about the tackle we use is a function of our search for delight in our fishing. The tastes we have in our fishing may appear to limit us in our methods, but at a deeper level they extend our personal pleasure in the sport.

CHAPTER FORTY

A Dilemma of Fly Lines

Thumbing through present day tackle catalogues, one's eye stops on the sections devoted to fly lines. I hear again the words of a rather exasperated tackle dealer as I look down the lists of types; 'There are far too many designs of fly line on the market.' Are there? Or ought the argument to be that there are far too many of the same kinds of line available, while the range of modern fly lines could well be extended to cover areas which many fly fishers feel are neglected by modern designs?

Most of us have little difficulty in reconstructing the recent history of the modern fly line. I was happily fishing silk lines in 1958, greasing when I wanted them to float and cleaning off grease when I wanted them to sink. Float they did, and, properly greased, they rode well, sitting high on the water on top of the surface film. My memories of summer dry fly fishing includes the delightful picture of dry fly fishing fast streams with the line snaking over the water, buoyant with floatant.

Sinking silk lines was another matter. Even the heaviest (my heaviest was a No. 6 salmon line) sank by settling down into the water. Often the bulk of a silk salmon line caused it to be washed away before it could be persuaded to reach the maximum depth. But one always, somehow, had an old silk line which seemed to sink faster than its well dressed younger brothers. I had an old brown silk, bought at a sale in Glasgow, and it dredged the bottom of many a loch for me in spring when I was trying out all sorts of deep nymphing tricks.

I saw and fished my first floater in Finland in 1958, and I also saw but did not fish, a sinking line from the same manufacturer. Both were level lines, and they did not attract me one bit. I thought them both crude. Who could fly fish with a floater with a thick end like that? I preferred to grease my silks and wait for plastic-coated lines to refine somewhat before I gave them a further trial.

Of course, within a season I fished a double tapered Air Cel, lent to me by Charlie McLaren when we were fishing together. I caught both salmon and trout on this line and became an enthusiast almost at once. I liked the way the line floated *in* the water rather than on it; I found the gentle sinking characteristics of the tip ideal for loch trouting. Since then I have fished this floater in several weights and tapers and I find its breeding proved season after season in both trout and salmon fishing.

The Wet Cel sinker came a season or so later and I found at once that it solved several of the problems of my fly fishing. It was a thin line, yet a heavy one and I found it cutting down through the water to fish light flies at good depth. If one was careful about line retrieval, remembering to handline in enough line, and to roll line up out of the water before lifting for the backcast, one could save a strained rod.

Fishing modern plastic dressed floaters and sinkers, however, became an either/or matter. Floaters were on top; sinkers were on the bottom, or were trying their best to get there. Silks would float well if greased well, but silks had the interesting quality of sinking slowly. With the modern line, mid-water fishing – especially for trout, had become impossible, or very difficult to carry out.

As a salmon fisher I found either top or bottom suited me. Mid-water is no-man's-land. Fish will rise to a mid-water fly, of course, but if you can interest them that much in your fly they will rise to the top layer of water just as readily. Really deep fish, such as springers, or autumn fish, respond well to the fly that hovers on the stones about their noses. These salmon are slow to move far for your fly in colder water. A mid-water fly would fail to move them.

In trout fishing, mid-water is quite different. Trout, of course, do rise to nymphs fished a couple of feet down, and I have known days on the loch when trout would only take flies down at this depth. Fast sinking lines rapidly go too deep in loch fishing, especially if any length of line is cast, and if you want to fish the cast out fairly slowly. With only floaters and sinkers available I have used the technique of the long leader with a floater to fish out this middle depth. But long leaders have their drawbacks, one of them being their failure to turn over well in casting. Another characteristic I dislike is that in playing a good fish to the net when you are alone there is difficulty in netting. A leader of a length greater than your rod always produces this problem.

In night sea trout fishing I have found the either/or characteristics of my fly lines useful. I have, over the seasons, however, become convinced that sea trout in the slower pools respond well to a deeply sunk fly, while those in the streamier pools with gravelly bottoms often insist on a surface-cutting wet fly which a floater fishes beautifully. But I have noted during lulls in night fishing on warm summer evenings, that the rod with a floater and a demon, fishing mid-water, usually takes a brace of fish after the surface plopping has stopped. In these circumstances it may well be that a mid-water wet fly would be ideal. Either/or may again be too stark a solution to the problem of fishing depth.

Recent catalogues now list a line to fill the vacancy. Sinkers are now fast or slow, with the slower sinking line suited to more or less the middle water fished at one time by wet silk. Are all our problems now history? I doubt it, but I am willing to try to prove my doubts to be mere sceptical whims.

I am somewhat worried by the way we are departing in our tackle from all-purpose gear, and with every advance we are introducing new specialisms. Three lines now do what one silk could have done (with the exception that silk failed to sink fast enough). Three six-guinea lines may not worry some anglers, but others would feel that they had spent their rent on tackle rather than on fishings. Further, my small niggle about the ends of modern fly lines being too thick begins to look like an argument for silk. I begin to doubt that plastic lines cast as well as silk. Perfectionists in accuracy casting use silk I hear. Plastic lines, casters say, do not turn over as silk does at the end of a long cast – at the vital presentation end.

But I am stopped in my nostalgic return to *some* of the qualities of silk when I think of long nights of sea trout fishing with modern floaters without problems of re-greasing a wet line in the dark. I remember too the way my deep sinkers have performed so well on sea trout in recent seasons, bringing the biggest and most exciting bags of fish I have ever had from certain waters which baffled me before. Further, I believe silk is becoming very difficult to obtain – only one British firm is still making lines of this sort. Perhaps I will after all add a slow sinker – a *c* belly – to my tackle, and carry a third rod with me to my fishing. And if the worst comes to the worst I can add a fourth reel, loaded with silk line, to my ridiculously bulging tackle bag!

Index